BibleTelling

INTERACTIVE BIBLE LEARNING

D1359879

CHOSEN CITY

CITY OF DAVID - NEHEMIAH

JOHN WALSH

Editorial services provided by Jan Walsh, International Learning Solutions
and George Rutherford, Rutherford Technical Consulting, Inc.
Cover and Interior design by Bradley S. Barth, Trace Design Studio, Inc.
Cover photography by Rick Kessinger
CD Production by Phillip Adams
Course Development Advisors: Dr. Mark Getz, Dr. Grant Lovejoy

A Teacher's Guide has been prepared for this book. For information,
go to www.BibleTelling.com

Library of Congress Cataloging-in-Publication Data

Walsh, John (John, D.), 1945—
        BibleTelling : Interactive Bible Learning ; Chosen City: City of David - Jeremiah / John Walsh.
ISBN: 1-933542-03-9
1. Christian Education. 2. Bible History. 3. Storytelling

Printed in the United States of America

CHOSEN CITY
CITY OF DAVID - NEHEMIAH

Name _____ Date _____

Table of Contents

INTERNATIONAL
LEARNING SOLUTIONS

2905 Gill Street - Bloomington, IL - 61704 - 800-420-0022

www.BibleTelling.com

A Message from the Storyteller

You have had quite an adventure if you have learned the stories in the first three books of this series. You have traveled through the Bible starting with creation. The world was destroyed with a flood, and then God chose a family to accomplish His purposes. We have followed Abraham's descendants through his son, grandson and great-grandchildren.

They went into Egypt where they later became slaves. God brought them out under the leadership of His servant, Moses. God established a lasting relationship with them and gave them His laws. It took them years of wandering before they finally took possession of the land promised to them. There, the chosen line once again went down through the years until it came to David.

This book begins with King David choosing a city to be the center for his kingdom. It is also the place God had chosen for His Temple. Therefore, this fourth book focuses on the chosen city and the Temple site.

It is a dramatic time in world history, as God raises up world kingdoms and mighty armies to accomplish His will. Jerusalem stands in the middle as great kings and fearless prophets come and go. The rulers of the world learn that God is the commander of the entire earth!

The Divided Kingdom – Israel & Judah

As you approach the stories in this fourth book, it is important to have a basic understanding of the Divided Kingdom. Here it is in a nutshell:

It begins with King Saul. He desperately wanted one of his sons to become the next king, but God had chosen David. When King Saul was killed in battle, all his hopes of a kingly line died with him. His three most capable sons were also killed, and the nation was left in confusion and turmoil. The big question was, "Who is the rightful king?" A division developed that eventually became two kingdoms.

Saul's top military general declared that Saul's last remaining son was king. The northern tribes of Israel sided with him. But the large and powerful tribe of Judah said their "favorite son" David should be king, and they gave him their allegiance. The first seven years of David's rule were over one part of a divided kingdom. In time the military general who had been against David changed his allegiance. The northern tribes agreed and the kingdom was once again united.

King David worked hard to strengthen this union. He treated all tribes as equal and moved his center of government to a neutral location. It was a place that was outside Judah, and a place that was not controlled by any particular tribe. It was a fortress called Jerusalem that was owned by the Jebusites. All the tribes could unite there without anyone feeling that the city belonged to them alone. It became known as the City of David.

David's son Solomon became king and was commissioned by God to build the Temple at Jerusalem. After Solomon died, his son was foolish, and the northern ten tribes rebelled. The nation was once again divided into two kingdoms. The northern ten tribes called themselves **Israel**. The little tribe of Benjamin joined the big tribe of Judah, and they called their kingdom **Judah**.

The northern ten tribes moved their center of government to the city of Samaria and selected another king. The new king felt strongly that one more thing needed to be done. He feared if the people continued going to Jerusalem to worship, they would eventually give their loyalty back to Judah. Therefore he set up another worship site and told the people it was "just as good as the Temple in Jerusalem."

Israel (the northern 10 tribes) quickly fell into idolatry and the people started worshiping false gods. After years of warning, God brought the Assyrian army against them. The Assyrians took the people of Israel away from their land and transported them elsewhere. They are now referred to as the "Lost Ten Tribes of Israel." The southern kingdom of Judah went through times of rebellion and repentance. They had righteous kings and wicked kings. God warned them of His judgment and sent His prophets to them time and again. When they completely turned their backs on God, they lost everything – their city, their land, and their Temple. The only thing they didn't lose was God's love and the hope of a future Kingdom.

David's kingly line continued on, and Jerusalem remains as "home" for the Jews even to this day.

Slow, Permanent Change

It is truly an adventure to learn God's stories, and I trust you are enjoying it. The ultimate goal of BibleTelling is to produce slow, permanent change within the lives of God's people. This takes place when people not only learn the story, but also internalize it into their lives.

The storyboards help you learn the story, but the activities are designed to bring the story into your inner person. At first glance, the activities may seem to be fun and frivolous but, in actuality, they are the key to making the story relate to your emotions and enjoyment.

Procedure for Learning a Story

Some may be joining this series for the first time. Therefore, let's review the procedure for learning the stories.

1. ## Read the story from the Bible.
   We provide activities called *Search the Scriptures* and *Scripture Crossword* that guide you through the story and emphasize important parts.

2. ## Read the cluster titles.
   Do not read the storyboard at this point, but simply read the cluster titles.

3. ## Listen to the story on the CD.
   Try to envision your own storyboard as you listen to the CD.

4. ## Study the storyboard until you can "see" the story.
   Take time to review the storyboard until you can see it in your mind. It is divided into three or four sections called "clusters." Freely change the storyboards so they make sense to you. Use hand gestures for every part, even if I don't suggest any.

5. ## Listen to the story a second time.
   You should be able to see the story in your mind as you listen to the story the second time. If not, review the storyboard again.

6. ## Tell the story in your own words.
   Don't wait until you know it better. Stumble through the story and tell it the best you can. Don't worry about trying to tell the story exactly as you hear it on the CD. Instead, tell it as you remember it. It becomes better each time you tell it.

7. ## Review the story every day.
   Listen to the story at a time most convenient to you. Some listen to it as they get ready in the morning, or as they go to work or school.

8. ## Tell the story to several people.
   Select people who are willing to listen to your story each week. Find those who are not overly critical and who are eager to hear the next story.

Let us hear from you!

Every day we receive word of more people growing in the knowledge of God and having their lives blessed and changed as they learn these stories from God's Word. These are people from Sunday School classes, Bible study groups, Christian schools, Bible colleges, homeschool families, seminaries, mission classes, and missionaries from around the world. Many of these folks have given us valuable input on things that will be helpful as we continue to develop future BibleTelling books.

If you have experiences to share, I would love to hear from you.

Contact me by email: jwalsh@ChristianStorytelling.com

John Walsh, President
Christian Storytelling Network

LESSON 28
CITY OF DAVID

CHOSEN CITY

JOHN WALSH

Search the Scriptures

Fill in the blanks

II SAMUEL 5:6-12

1. David and his men went to _____ which was inhabited by the _____.

2. David's men conquered the _____ of Zion.

3. From that time on, David lived there and he called it the _____.

4. David became _____ because God was with him.

5. Hiram, the king of Tyre, provided workers and _____ trees to build a _____ for David.

II SAMUEL 6:1-11

6. David decided to take his men and go get the _____ from the house of Abinadab.

7. They set the Ark of God on a _____ that was pulled by _____.

8. The two sons of Abinadab, _____ and _____, drove the cart.

9. As their procession moved along, David and the Israelites celebrated unto the Lord in what way? _____.

10. When the oxen shook the cart, _____ put out his hand and touched the Ark to steady it.

11. What happened to Uzzah? _____

12. How did David respond? _____

13. What did David do with the Ark of God? _____

14. The Ark of God was in the house of _____ for _____ months.

15. During that time, the Lord _____ Obed-Edom and all his household.

II SAMUEL 6:12-18

16. When David heard of the great blessing, he once again decided to bring the Ark of God up to _____.

17. After the men carrying the ark had gone a certain distance, David _____ unto the Lord.

18. What other things took place as the people moved along with the Ark of God? _____ _____

19. When they reached the City of David, they set the _____ in its place in the tabernacle (tent) that David had prepared for it.

II SAMUEL 7:1-17

20. David said to _____ the prophet, "I dwell in a house of _____, but the Ark of God dwells in _____."

21. The prophet said, "Go, do _____, for the Lord is with you."

22. That _____ the word of the _____ came to Nathan with a message for David.

God's Message for David given through Nathan the prophet.

23. "Ever since I brought up the Israelites out of Egypt, My presence has been with them in a _____. Have I asked you to build me a _____ of cedar?"

24. "I took you from following the _____ to be a _____ over Israel; I have been with you and I have given you rest from all your _____."

25. "I will make your name _____, and I will appoint a place for my people _____ where they can live and not be _____."

26. "When your life is over, I will set up your son and I will establish his _____. He shall build a _____ for Me."

27. "I will be a _____ to him and he will be my _____."

28. "Thus, your house and your kingdom shall be established _____."

I CHRONICLES 22:6-11

29. David said that the Lord would not use him to build His house because he had shed much _____ on the earth and he waged great _____.

30. God said He would give Solomon _____ from all his _____, and He would give to Israel _____ and _____ during Solomon's reign.

The City of David

• When David became king, Jerusalem was a small city controlled by the Jebusites. It was a walled fortress built on Mount Zion.

• David's army conquered the stronghold by getting inside the walls through the water tunnels.

• It was renamed "The City of David," and from that time on it was the center of King David's government.

• Even today the City of David remains as a distinct part of Jerusalem.

Scripture Crossword

II Samuel 5:6-12, II Samuel 6:1-18, II Samuel 7:1-17 I Chronicles 22: 6-11

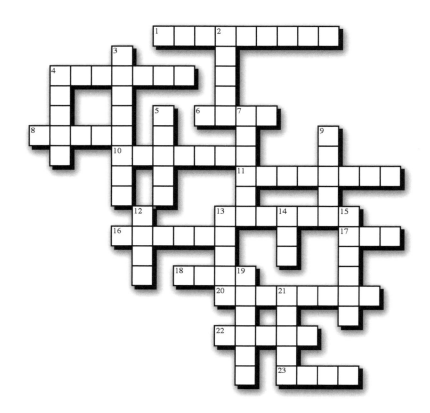

ACROSS

1 The Jebusites lived in this city.
4 David charged ___ to build a house for the Lord.
6 Brother of Uzzah
8 Kind of wood used for David's palace
10 God told David his throne would be established ___.
11 Uzzah's father
13 The Lord ___ Obed-Edom's household while the ark was there.
16 Who was watching David from a window?
17 Brought to the City of David
18 The walled fortress was on Mt. ___.
20 Michal was Saul's ___.
22 The Ark of the Lord stayed at Obed-Edom's house for how many months?
23 Place where Ark was put

DOWN

2 God struck him dead.
3 David became more ___ because the Lord was with him.
4 David's first occupation, caring for ___.
5 King of Tyre
7 David was the king of ___.
9 God said He would grant Israel ___ and quiet during Solomon's reign.
12 Jerusalem is also called the ___ of David.
13 Much ___ was shed by David.
14 God said of Solomon, "He will be my ___."
15 David ___ before the Lord with all his might.
19 Prophet who spoke with David
21 God's message to David: "I will make your name ___."

Storyboard

Study the Storyboard until you can "see" the story

This story tells about the three possessions God gave David:
(1) an eternal city, (2) the Ark of God, and (3) an eternal blessing.

When telling a story, dress in a way that causes your listeners to focus on your face.

FIRST CLUSTER – Eternal City

This section of the story is very simple and is not hard to remember. Jerusalem is a stronghold built on Mt Zion. David's army captures it by using underground water tunnels. It becomes the City of David.

> *When David became king, Jerusalem was a small city controlled by the Jebusites. It was a walled fortress on Mount Zion. David's army conquered it by getting inside the walls through the water tunnels. He renamed it "The City of David," and from that time on it was the center of his government.*
> *God was with David and established his kingdom over Israel. The Lord made him more and more powerful and gave him victory over all his enemies.*

SECOND CLUSTER – Ark of God

This cluster contains three happenings – moving the Ark improperly, blessing the family where it is stored, moving the Ark properly.

(1) In the first part, the people are doing a good thing, but ignoring God's instructions. Picture a new cart being pulled by oxen. People are rejoicing until a man gets killed.

(2) In the second part, David is confused, so he stores the Ark with a family for three months. God blesses the family, which catches David's attention.

(3) In the third part, the Ark is moved properly and successfully. David makes sacrifices, blesses the people, and feeds them.

> *The King decided to bring the Ark of God to Jerusalem. His men put it onto a new cart pulled by oxen. This was not how God said it was to be moved. David and the people walked along as the cart moved toward Jerusalem. They celebrated, sang songs, and played instruments. At one point the oxen shook the cart, and a man reached out to steady it. As soon as his hand touched the Ark, God struck him dead!*
> *David was shocked and confused. He said, "How can the Ark of God ever get to Jerusalem?" He asked a family who lived nearby to store it. It remained there for three months, and the Lord greatly blessed that family.*
> *King David heard how God was blessing that family, so once again he decided to bring the Ark to Jerusalem. This time, he moved it properly. Poles were put through rings that were on the Ark so the priests could carry it on their shoulders. A sacrifice was made to the Lord, and the people shouted for joy and blew trumpets as the Ark of God moved toward Jerusalem.*
> *When they reached Jerusalem, David placed the Ark in a tent that he had prepared for it. More sacrifices were made to the Lord, and he blessed the people. He gave every person — both men and women — something to eat and then he sent them to their homes.*

THIRD CLUSTER – Eternal Blessing

David wanted to provide a nicer place for God to dwell. He asked the prophet if he could build the Temple for God. The prophet said yes, but God said no.

God uses this occasion to give David His eternal blessing. He tells David about his past, present, and future. God then tells him how His house was to be built. You can remember this by envisioning the following picture.

Past – David's Background
Envision a shepherd boy with a crown on his head.
- shepherd   You were following sheep.
- king   I made you king of Israel.

Present – David's Surroundings
The enemies of the shepherd boy are now sitting peacefully around him.
- victory   I have given you victory over your enemies.

Future – David's future
The shepherd boy has his name on his chest, in big print. Other kings come up to stand with him (his royal line).
- name   I will establish your name among the greatest men who will ever live.
- family line   Your royal family line will last forever.

Future – God's house
The shepherd boy becomes a man of war, with a sword in his hand. His son stands next to him with a hammer in his hand. David then put his son's hand into God's hand (God becomes his father).
- reason   You are a man of war, and many have died because of you.
- house   Your son…will build My house.
- child   I will be a father to him and establish his kingdom

Practice this mental picture until you can easily associate it with the story.

As the years went by, the king became settled in his palace and the Lord gave him rest from all of the nations that fought against him. David's mind turned to the idea of building a Temple for the Lord. He said to his prophet, "I am living in a beautiful palace, while the Ark of God remains in a tent!"

The prophet agreed, saying, "Go ahead and build the Temple. God will be pleased."

That night the Lord gave the prophet a message for David. "Did I ask you to build a house for Me? You were following sheep when I made you king of Israel. I have been with you all these years, and have given you victory over your enemies. Now I will establish your name among the greatest men who will ever live. Your royal family line will last forever.

Still, you will not build My house. I have made you a man of war and many have died because of you. Your son will be a man of peace, and he will build My house. I will be a father to him and establish his kingdom."

King David was content when he heard this message, and he humbled himself before the Lord.

Telling the Story

THE CITY OF DAVID

When David became king, Jerusalem was a small city controlled by the Jebusites. It was a walled fortress on Mount Zion. David's army conquered it by getting inside the walls through the water tunnels. He renamed it "The City of David," and from that time on it was the center of his government.

God was with David and established his kingdom over Israel. The Lord made him more and more powerful and gave him victory over all his enemies.

The King decided to bring the Ark of God to Jerusalem. His men put it onto a new cart pulled by oxen. This was not how God said it was to be moved. David and the people walked along as the cart moved toward Jerusalem. They celebrated, sang songs, and played instruments. At one point the oxen shook the cart, and a man reached out to steady it. As soon as his hand touched the Ark, God struck him dead!

David was shocked and confused. He said, "How can the Ark of God ever get to Jerusalem?" He asked a family who lived nearby to store it. It remained there for three months, and the Lord greatly blessed that family.

King David heard how God was blessing that family, so once again he decided to bring the Ark to Jerusalem. This time, he moved it properly. Poles were put through rings that were on the Ark so the priests could carry it on their shoulders. A sacrifice was made to the Lord, and the people shouted for joy and blew trumpets as the Ark of God moved toward Jerusalem.

When they reached Jerusalem, David placed the Ark in a tent that he had prepared for it. More sacrifices were made to the Lord, and he blessed the people. He gave every person – both men and women – something to eat and then he sent them to their homes.

As the years went by, the king became settled in his palace and the Lord gave him rest from all of the nations that fought against him. David's mind turned to the idea of building a Temple for the Lord. He said to his prophet, "I am living in a beautiful palace, while the Ark of God remains in a tent!"

The prophet agreed, saying, "Go ahead and build the Temple. God will be pleased."

That night the Lord gave the prophet a message for David. "Did I ask you to build a house for Me? You were following sheep when I made you king of Israel. I have been with you all these years, and have given you victory over your enemies. Now I will establish your name among the greatest men who will ever live. Your royal family line will last forever.

Still, you will not build My house. I have made you a man of war and many have died because of you. Your son will be a man of peace, and he will build My house. I will be a father to him and establish his kingdom."

King David was content when he heard this message, and he humbled himself before the Lord.

Extra Storyboard

First
Cluster

Second
Cluster

Third
Cluster

Activities

Using the boxes below, give the storyboard in words or pictures.

First Cluster	Second Cluster	Third Cluster

Feel free to use blank pages to write down or draw additional clusters or ideas.

What did you learn about **God** from *The City of David?*

_____

_____

_____

What did you learn about **people** from *The City of David?*

_____

_____

_____

What was your **favorite** part of the story? Tell why.

_____

_____

_____

PROVERB: a pithy statement that helps you remember an important truth. Create a proverb based on this story.

_____

_____

BANNER OR BUMPER STICKER: Give the essence of this story in six words or less.

_____

ACTIVITIES: Choose from the following, or create another activity that helps you learn the story.

Drama
- Act out the part of the story about moving the Ark to the City of David.
- Have one person tell God's message and promises to David, while several others pantomime each part.

Storytelling
- Do a "Good News" and "Bad News" story that includes all three parts of this lesson. Have at least two tellers who toss the story back and forth. Coach listeners to respond with appropriate verbal or facial expressions.

Music
- Create a marching song such as might be sung with joy while traveling along toward a place of great anticipation. Perform the song and use instruments to accompany your march.

Art
- Draw a picture of one or more scenes in this story.

Craft
- Look up information about the Stronghold of Zion and build a model of it including the water tunnels.

Craft & Storytelling
- Put together a "Photo Album" showing highlights of David's life. Have "Grandpa David" show the album to his grandchild and tell highlights of his life.

Food
- Look up information about the food David gave the people and prepare some for the class. II Sam. 6:19

Research
- How did David's army get into the Jebusite stronghold (Jerusalem) by using the water tunnels?
- What were God's exact instructions for the proper way to move the Ark from place to place?

Discussion
- Why do you think Uzzah's punishment was so severe?

TIE TO PREVIOUS STORY: Write how you would connect this story with the previous story.

_____

_____

_____

TELL THE STORY: To whom did you tell the story and what was their response?

_____

_____

_____

Quiz 28

Name _____

Date _____

MATCHING

____ 1. Zion   a. provided access to the stronghold

____ 2. Jebusites   b. father of Uzzah and Ahio

____ 3. water shaft   c. brought from caring for sheep to being ruler over Israel

____ 4. Solomon   d. died when he touched the Ark of God

____ 5. David   e. was put on a new cart to be taken to Jerusalem

____ 6. Uzzah   f. his household was blessed by the presence of the Ark

____ 7. Ark of God   g. heir to David's throne

____ 8. Hiram, King of Tyre   h. a stronghold

____ 9. Nathan   i. original inhabitants of Jerusalem

____ 10. Abinadab   j. place where David kept the Ark of God

____ 11. Obed-Edom   k. provided workers and materials to build David's house

____ 12. tabernacle (tent)   l. prophet

MULTIPLE CHOICE

____ 13. David's house was made of _____.

   a. animal skins   b. gold   c. cedar

____ 14. As the Ark was being moved to Jerusalem, those who accompanied it _____.

   a. wept   b. played instruments   c. prayed

____ 15. When the Ark reached the City of David, it was placed in _____.

   a. a tent   b. the Temple   c. the center of the city

____ 16. God did not choose to have David build His house, because David was _____.

   a. unwilling   b. a man of war   c. without resources

____ 17. David's _____ was the one God would use to build the temple.

   a. father   b. brother   c. son

____ 18. God said He would give Solomon _____ his enemies.

   a. victory over   b. rest from   c. revenge on

____ 19. God said He would give Israel _____ during Solomon's reign.

   a. peace   b. famine   c. abundant crops

____ 20. God said David's kingdom would be established _____.

   a. for many years   b. until his death   c. forever

(5 points each question)   SCORE _____

LESSON 29

NUMBERING THE PEOPLE

CHOSEN CITY

JOHN WALSH

Search the Scriptures

Fill in the blanks

I CHRONICLES 21:1-19

1. David told Joab to count how many people were in _____.

2. How did Joab feel about this idea? _____

3. Joab counted _____ armed men in Israel and _____ armed men in Judah.

4. _____ was displeased when David ordered the "numbering" of the people.

5. David admitted his sin and asked God to _____.

6. The Lord spoke to _____, David's seer (prophet) and gave him a message for David.

7. God offered David _____ different punishments and told him to _____ for himself which he would have.

8. The choices were: (1) three years of _____, (2) three months of being _____ by Israel's enemies, or (3) three days of a _____ in the land.

9. David chose to "fall into the hand of the Lord" because _____.

10. The Lord sent a plague upon Israel, and _____ men died.

11. God sent _____ to destroy Jerusalem, but he stopped when he came to the _____ of Ornan (Araunah) the Jebusite.

12. David pleaded with God to _____ punishing Israel for his sin.

13. The angel said that David should go and _____ on the threshing floor of Ornan the Jebusite.

I CHRONICLES 21:19-27

14. When David asked to _____ Ornan's threshing floor, Ornan offered to _____ it to David.

15. King David said he wanted to buy it at _____ price because he didn't want to take what belonged to _____ and give offerings to God of that which _____.

16. So David _____ the threshing floor and built an _____ there.

17. He offered _____ offerings and _____ offerings and called on the Lord.

18. The Lord answered him by sending _____ on the offerings and telling the angel to put his _____ back in its _____.

I CHRONICLES 22:1-5

19. David declared that the place where he had sacrificed and the Lord answered him was "the _____ of the Lord God."

20. He commanded workers to bring huge supplies of stones, _____, bronze, and _____ logs in preparation for _____ the house of the Lord.

21. David made abundant preparations for Solomon's temple before his _____.

II CHRONICLES 3:1

22. The threshing floor of Ornan was located at Mount _____, where Abraham offered up Isaac to God (Genesis 22), and where _____ later built the House of the Lord (temple).

Scripture Crossword

I Chronicles 21:1-27, I Chronicles 22:1-5, II Chronicles 3:1

ACROSS

1 "I will not sacrifice to the Lord that which costs me _____."

4 One of the tribes Joab did not count

7 ___ thousand men died in the plague on Israel.

9 commanded by David to take the census

11 David chose to fall into the hands of the ___ for his punishment.

13 How many sons did Ornan (Araunah) have?

14 The angel of the Lord ordered David to build this.

15 one of David's options for punishment

17 God punished ___ for David's sin.

18 David compared the people of Israel to this animal.

20 David said to God, "I have ___ greatly!"

22 one of the tribes Joab did not count

23 purchased by David

DOWN

2 God gave David this many choices for his punishment.

3 David and the elders were clothed in what?

4 David offered to ___ the threshing floor.

5 The people of Tyre brought ___ logs for the temple.

6 David's seer

8 David made preparations for this before his death.

9 God sent an angel to destroy this city.

10 What was Ornan(Araunah) threshing?

12 How God felt about David numbering the people.

14 What did David see standing between heaven and earth?

16 David said about God, "His _____ are great."

17 The nails for the temple were made out of what?

18 David's son

19 The temple was built on Mount ___.

21 David insisted on paying __ price for the threshing floor.

Storyboard

Study the Storyboard until you can "see" the story

FIRST CLUSTER – Numbering the People

This part of the story is fairly simple to remember. David calls Joab and tells him to number the people. Joab holds up his hands and says, "Don't do it!" David is determined, so Joab starts numbering. 1,500,000.

King David called for Joab, who was the commander of his army. He said, "Go throughout the land – from the north to the south – to every tribe – and number all the people."

Joab knew that God did not want David to do this. He said, "The Lord will give you as many people as you need for any situation. Don't hurt them by disobeying God." But David insisted, so Joab had to do what he was told.

He used his army to go to every part of Israel and record the number of people. When they were finished, Joab told David he had over 1,500,000 men who were able to go to war if needed.

SECOND CLUSTER – Judgment

David realizes what he has done, so he prays for forgiveness. God's prophet holds up three fingers (3 years, 3 months, and 3 days). "Famine for three years, the swords of your enemies for three months, or the Sword of the Lord for three days." David looks terrified, but he has to choose. He doesn't even consider option one, but only thinks about options two and three. He finally decides he would rather suffer under God's hand rather than under the hands men.

Picture the Angel of the Lord bringing an epidemic upon the land. 70,000 people die. The angel turns towards Jerusalem, and God says, "enough." The angel stops over the threshing floor.

After David heard this report, he was troubled in his heart. He knew the Lord was displeased with him. He prayed, "Oh God, I have sinned against You, and acted foolishly. Please forgive my sin."

The Lord sent a message to David through His prophet. He said, "You are to choose one of three punishments for this sin. The first is a three-year famine, which will devastate the land. The second is to be chased by your enemies for three months, and you will lose battle after battle. The third is to face the Sword of the Lord for three days, and a severe epidemic will sweep across the land."

David looked at the prophet in shock. Finally he said, "All three of these terrify me! Still, I choose to suffer under the hand of God, rather than suffering at the hands of men. I know the Lord is full of mercy."

So God brought a severe epidemic upon Israel. He sent the angel of the Lord, who swept across the land, and 70,000 men died. The angel then focused on Jerusalem. As death came upon the city, the Lord stopped him and said, "It is enough! Hold back your hand." The angel stopped immediately. He was at the place where Abraham offered up Isaac to the Lord, which was a threshing floor owned by a Jebusite named Ornan.

THIRD CLUSTER – The Threshing Floor

This cluster has three parts – the fierce angel, the negotiation, and the offering.

(1) Picture the threshing floor with the angel standing above it. Several people are bowing down – David, the elders, Ornan, and his four sons. David prays and the prophet walks up with the answer.

(2) David immediately walks towards the place that has a fierce angel hovering over the top. Ornan also goes there and the two talk. This is an important conversation because this is where David buys the future Temple site.

(3) An altar is built, wood put in place, the oxen killed and placed on top. God brings fire down and burns the offering. The angel puts his sword away and the epidemic stops. Before we end the story, we look at the threshing floor and realize it is an important spot.

David looked up and saw the angel standing above the threshing floor. He held a sword in his hand, which was stretched out over the city. Ornan and his four sons also saw the angel and hid themselves. David and the elders of Israel fell to their knees and put their faces to the ground.

David cried out to God. "Oh Lord, I am the one who sinned! I am the one who did wrong! Not these people who are like sheep – what have they done? Let Your judgment fall on me and my family."

The prophet once again approached David with a message from God. "Build an altar to the Lord on the threshing floor of Ornan, the Jebusite." David immediately walked toward the threshing floor. When Ornan saw him coming, he went and bowed down before the king.

David lifted him up and said, "Allow me to buy your threshing floor to build an altar to the Lord so He will hold back the plague from the people. I will pay you the full price for it."

Ornan said, "Oh king, I gladly give you all you need for the sacrifice. Build your altar and take these oxen for the burnt offering. Use the wood for the fire and the wheat for a grain offering. I give it all to you. I just pray the Lord will hear your request."

David looked at him. "No my friend, I will buy it all from you at the full price. I will not make a sacrifice to the Lord using that which costs me nothing." So David bought the threshing floor, the oxen, and the wood. He then built the altar and made his offering to the Lord.

God heard David's prayer and brought down fire from heaven to consume the offering. He then commanded the angel, "Put your sword back in its sheath!" With that, the epidemic was over.

From that day on, David offered his sacrifices to the Lord upon that altar. He declared, "This is the house of the Lord." Then he organized people and nations to bring all the materials needed for building a magnificent Temple. Years later, Solomon built the Temple of the Lord at that place.

Telling the Story

NUMBERING THE PEOPLE

King David called for Joab, who was the commander of his army. He said, "Go throughout the land – from the north to the south – to every tribe – and number all the people."

Joab knew that God did not want David to do this. He said, "The Lord will give you as many people as you need for any situation. Don't hurt them by disobeying God." But David insisted, so Joab had to do what he was told. He used his army to go to every part of Israel and record the number of people. When they were finished, Joab told David he had over 1,500,000 men who were able to go to war if needed.

After David heard this report, he was troubled in his heart. He knew the Lord was displeased with him. He prayed, "Oh God, I have sinned against You, and acted foolishly. Please forgive my sin."

The Lord sent a message to David through His prophet. He said, "You are to choose one of three punishments for this sin. The first is a three-year famine, which will devastate the land. The second is to be chased by your enemies for three months, and you will lose battle after battle. The third is to face the Sword of the Lord for three days, and a severe epidemic will sweep across the land."

David looked at the prophet in shock. Finally he said, "All three of these terrify me! Still, I choose to suffer under the hand of God, rather than suffering at the hands of men. I know the Lord is full of mercy."

So God brought a severe epidemic upon Israel. He sent the angel of the Lord, who swept across the land, and 70,000 men died. The angel then focused on Jerusalem. As death came upon the city, the Lord stopped him and said, "It is enough! Hold back your hand." The angel stopped immediately. He was at the place where Abraham offered up Isaac to the Lord, which was a threshing floor owned by a Jebusite named Ornan.

David looked up and saw the angel standing above the threshing floor. He held a sword in his hand, which was stretched out over the city. Ornan and his four sons also saw the angel and hid themselves. David and the elders of Israel fell to their knees and put their faces to the ground.

David cried out to God. "Oh Lord, I am the one who sinned! I am the one who did wrong! Not these people who are like sheep – what have they done? Let Your judgment fall on me and my family."

The prophet once again approached David with a message from God. "Build an altar to the Lord on the threshing floor of Ornan, the Jebusite." David immediately walked toward the threshing floor. When Ornan saw him coming, he went and bowed down before the king.

David lifted him up and said, "Allow me to buy your threshing floor to build an altar to the Lord so He will hold back the plague from the people. I will pay you the full price for it."

Ornan said, "Oh king, I gladly give you all you need

for the sacrifice. Build your altar and take these oxen for the burnt offering. Use the wood for the fire and the wheat for a grain offering. I give it all to you. I just pray the Lord will hear your request."

David looked at him. "No, my friend, I will buy it all from you at the full price. I will not make a sacrifice to the Lord using that which costs me nothing." So David bought the threshing floor, the oxen, and the wood. He then built the altar and made his offering to the Lord.

God heard David's prayer and brought down fire from heaven to consume the offering. He then commanded the angel, "Put your sword back in its sheath!" With that, the epidemic was over.

From that day on, David offered his sacrifices to the Lord upon that altar. He declared, "This is the house of the Lord." Then he organized people and nations to bring all the materials needed for building a magnificent Temple. Years later, Solomon built the Temple of the Lord at that place.

You have probably seen the place where Ornan's threshing floor was located if you watch television news. When you see a news report on Jerusalem, it usually shows a picture of the Dome of the Rock. That is where the Temple was located, where Ornan had his threshing floor, and where Abraham built an altar and offered up Isaac.

Activities

Using the boxes below, give the storyboard in words or pictures.

First Cluster	Second Cluster	Third Cluster

Feel free to use blank pages to write down or draw additional clusters or ideas.

What did you learn about **God** from the story of *Numbering the People?*

_____

_____

_____

What did you learn about **people** from the story of *Numbering the People?*

_____

_____

_____

What was your **favorite** part of the story? Tell why.

_____

_____

_____

PROVERB: a pithy statement that helps you remember an important truth. Create a proverb based on this story.

_____

_____

BANNER OR BUMPER STICKER: Give the essence of this story in six words or less.

ACTIVITIES: Choose from the following, or create another activity that helps you learn the story.

Drama
- Have a "therapist" interview the various characters in this story and talk about how they felt at different points in the story.
- Act out all that happens while the Angel stood with his sword lifted up, until God told him, "Put your sword back in its sheath!"

Dramatic Dialogue
- Have a discussion between David and his prophet concerning the three options for punishment.

Storytelling
- Use puppets to dramatize the conversations between David and Joab, David and God, David and the prophet, David and Ornan, God and the Angel.
- Evening News: Reporter tells the story while characters are silently acting it out.

Poetry
- Write a story-poem about King David numbering the people and the events that resulted.

Art
- Draw a picture showing how you envision the most memorable scene from this story.
- Draw a series of pictures to show the events of this story in the order they took place.

Research
- A key emphasis in this story is on a particular piece of ground. Trace the ownership of this plot of land, and how it ties in to current events and the Dome of the Rock
- What was known about Jerusalem when Abraham offered Isaac on Mt. Moriah? What was its name? What famous king did they have before David? How close was the town to Mt. Moriah when Abraham and Isaac were there?

Discussion
- Why was it a bad thing for David to number the people?
- What would have happened if David had chosen a different punishment?
- What other Bible characters expressed a willingness to sacrifice themselves to save their people?

TIE TO PREVIOUS STORY: Write how you would connect this story with the previous story.

_____

_____

_____

TELL THE STORY: To whom did you tell the story and what was their response?

_____

_____

_____

Quiz 29

Name _____

MULTIPLE CHOICE

Date _____

____ 1. David told his army captain to _____ all the people in Israel.
    a. speak to   b. count   c. give weapons to

____ 2. Altogether there were over _____ men who could fight.
    a. 500,000   b. 1,500,000   c. 6,000,000

____ 3. David's decision to number the people _____ the Lord.
    a. pleased   b. displeased   c. surprised

____ 4. The Lord sent a message to David through his _____.
    a. son   b. wife   c. seer

____ 5. God said He would give David the choice between _____ different punishments.
    a. three   b. five   c. seven

____ 6. David chose to suffer at the hand of _____.
    a. the Lord   b. Satan   c. his enemies

____ 7. When God sent a plague on Israel, _____ men died.
    a. 30,000   b. 50,000   c. 70,000

____ 8. God's angel of death stopped when he came to the _____ of Ornan the Jebusite.
    a. threshing floor   b. harvest fields   c. grinding house

____ 9. David pleaded with God to _____ His punishment of Israel.
    a. continue   b. begin   c. stop

____ 10. David asked God to let His punishment fall on _____.
    a. him and his family   b. his army commander c. the Jebusites

____ 11. The angel told David to go and build _____ on Ornan's threshing floor.
    a. an altar   b. a gallows   c. a memorial

____ 12. David asked Ornan to _____ the threshing floor.
    a. loan him   b. sell him   c. clean

____ 13. When David offered sacrifices and called on the Lord, God answered by sending _____.
    a. clouds   b. rain   c. fire

____ 14. God told the angel to put his sword _____.
    a. on the ground   b. on the altar   c. back in its sheath

____ 15. David declared that the place where God met with him was the _____.
    a. gate of heaven   b. house of the Lord   c. rock of his salvation

____ 16. David commanded gold, silver, iron, bronze and wood brought for _____.
    a. waging a war   b. building a temple   c. sacrificing to the Lord.

____ 17. David made abundant preparations before _____.
    a. his son was born   b. his coronation   c. his death

____ 18. The threshing floor of Ornan was on Mount _____.
    a. Moriah   b. Sinai   c. Pisgah

____ 19. Who said, "I have sinned greatly. I have done foolishly!" ?
    a. Joab   b. David   c. Gad

____ 20. Who said, "I will not sacrifice to God that which costs me nothing." ?
    a. Jonathan   b. David   c. Solomon

(5 points each question)

SCORE _____

LESSON 30

SOLOMON

CHOSEN CITY

JOHN WALSH

Search the Scriptures

Fill in the blanks

I KINGS 3:5-28

1. God appeared to Solomon in a dream and said, "_____."

2. Solomon asked for a/an _____ heart to rule the Lord's people.

3. How did God feel about Solomon's request? _____

4. God said He would grant Solomon's request, and He would also give him _____ and _____.

5. If Solomon would walk in God's ways and keep His commandments, God would_____.

6. Two _____ came to King Solomon with two _____ – one dead and the other alive.

7. When each woman claimed the _____ child, Solomon said, " Bring me a _____."

8. Then he commanded _____ and give _____ to each woman."

9. Solomon gave the living child to the woman who _____.

10. All Israel saw that the _____ of God was in Solomon.

I KINGS 4:30-34

11. Solomon's wisdom caused his fame to spread throughout all the surrounding _____.

12. Solomon authored three thousand _____ and more than a thousand _____.

13. He was also an expert on _____, animals, _____, creeping things, and _____.

14. People and kings from other nations came to hear the _____ of Solomon.

I KINGS 6:1-7, 14-38

15. Solomon began to build the Temple _____ years after the Israelites came out of the land of Egypt.

16. No hammers or other tools were _____ in the Temple while it was being built.

17. The inside walls were made of _____, and the floors were made of _____.

18. Solomon made an inner sanctuary for the Ark of God and covered it with pure _____.

19. Solomon's Temple took _____ years to build.

I KINGS 8:1-14

20. Solomon called together all the elders of Israel, and the priests brought the _____
    from the tabernacle (tent) where it had been kept, and they set it in the _____.

21. When the priests came out of the Most Holy Place, a _____ filled the House of the Lord.

22. Then King Solomon _____ the whole assembly of Israel.

I KINGS 9:1-9

23. The Lord said if Solomon would do all that God commanded, his kingdom would be established
    _____.

24. But if Solomon or his descendants turned away and served other_____, there would be awful results:

    • The people of Israel would be taken out of their _____.

    • God would remove Himself from the _____ .

    • People who passed by the Temple would _____

Scripture Crossword

I KINGS 3:5-28, I KINGS 4:30-34, I KINGS 6:1-38, I KINGS 8:1-14, I KINGS 9:1-9

ACROSS

6 The only things in the Ark of the Lord were two stone ___.
8 The temple walls were covered with this wood.
10 In order to end the argument between the women, the king asked for a ___.
11 God promised Solomon both riches and ___.
13 Solomon overlaid the inner sanctuary with pure ___.
14 place where the Lord appeared to Solomon in a dream
15 The ___ carried the ark of the Lord.
17 No sounds of ___ were heard at the temple building site.
19 In the inner sanctuary were a pair of ___.
20 Singular form of cherubim
21 King Solomon ___ the assembly of Israel.

DOWN

1 Solomon's father
2 The ___ of the Temple was made of cypress.
3 Two women were arguing over a ___.
4 Solomon wrote over ___ thousand songs.
5 All Israel saw that Solomon was filled with ___.
6 Solomon wrote ___ thousand proverbs.
7 People came from afar to hear the wisdom of ___.
8 After the priests moved the Ark into the Most Holy Place, a ___ filled the temple.
9 God told Solomon to ___ for whatever he wanted.
12 The doors leading to the inner sanctuary were made of this wood.
13 The Israelites were not to worship other ___.
15 Solomon's request ___ the Lord.
16 Solomon spent how many years building the temple?
17 House of the Lord
18 Solomon called himself a "___ child"

Storyboard

Study the Storyboard until you can "see" the story

FIRST CLUSTER – Solomon Asks for Wisdom

Solomon became king of Israel, and God asked him what he wanted. Solomon was nervous about following his father, who was a great king. He didn't feel adequate for the job. He was being asked to lead the people of God. Remember this by envisioning Solomon pointing to his father, pointing at himself, and pointing to all the people around him.

Solomon asks for understanding and God is pleased. He could have asked for long life, riches, or peace (security). To remember these, envision an old man with expensive jewelry around him. He has a peaceful look on his face.

God gives him all three, but there is a requirement for long life. He has to follow God for his entire life.

> The name Solomon means "peaceful." It is derived from the Hebrew word **shalom,** meaning "peace".

Before David died, he made his son Solomon king of Israel. Solomon loved the Lord and tried to follow the example of his father. One day, the Lord appeared to him and asked, "What do you want Me to give you?"

Without hesitation, Solomon said, "Lord, my father was a great king, and I feel like a child who doesn't know anything. Yet, You have placed me over Your great people. If You will give me one thing, give me the understanding to rule them wisely."

The Lord was pleased with Solomon's answer. "You have asked for wisdom instead of long life, riches, or peace. Therefore I will give you wisdom like no one has ever had or ever will have. In addition I will also give you riches and honor. And – if you continue to follow Me like your father did – I will also give you long life."

SECOND CLUSTER – Solomon Uses Wisdom

This section is "a story within a story," and it is easy to remember. There are two women, each with a newborn baby boy. One baby dies in the night, and both women say it was the other's son. No one knows which son died except these two women, but both claim the son who is alive. Solomon solves the mystery by threatening to cut the living child in half.

The end of this cluster sums up Solomon's growth in wisdom. Four statements are made about it.
- The people knew God had given wisdom to the king.
- He increased in wisdom and wrote proverbs and songs.
- People traveled to Israel to hear his wisdom.
- God gave wealth & peace to Israel.

Soon after this promise, two women came before Solomon with a complaint against each other. One said, "This woman and I live in the same house. I gave birth to a son, and three days later she gave birth to a son. While we were sleeping, she accidentally rolled over on her son and killed him. In the night, she took my child from beside me and put her dead son in his place. When I awoke in the morning to nurse my son, the child was dead. I then realized it was not my son at all, but hers. She has my child."

The other woman said, "No, the living child is mine and the dead one is hers!" The two began arguing in front of the king.

He turned to a guard and said, "Come here with a sword." Then pointing to the child, he said, "Divide the child in two and give each mother a half."

One woman cried out, "No, don't kill my son! She can have him! Please let him live."

The other woman said, "Yes, cut the child in half, so we both will have a part."

The king turned to the guard, "Give the child to the first woman. I know she is the mother because her heart cries out for the child."

When Israel heard this, they knew God had given wisdom to Solomon. He increased in wisdom over the years and wrote proverbs and songs. People came from other countries to hear him speak words of wisdom. God also gave Solomon great wealth.

THIRD CLUSTER – Solomon Builds the Temple

Solomon built the Temple of God, and it became the center of activity for the rest of the Bible. Present-day news talks about the site where it sat, and God says it will be rebuilt in our future. You are about to learn the story of how it was first built.

The events that surround the building project can be divided into three happenings – construction of the Temple, the dedication service, and God's warning to Solomon.

(1) To remember the construction, envision a work crew who picks up wood and big stones. Behind them is the number 480, and the number 7 is in front of them. They walk quietly around the building site while they put the wood inside the building. Oh, don't forget the gold.

(2) To remember the dedication, envision all the leaders of Israel getting together as the Ark goes into the Temple. They look up when the Glory of the Lord comes down. Before they go home, the king stands up, blesses them and dedicates the building to God.

(3) It is important to remember God's warning because you will see it fulfilled in the story of Jeremiah.

God gives two positives and three negatives.

(+) I have sanctified the Temple. I will establish your kingdom if you obey.

(–) If you (or your sons) don't obey:

  • I will take Israel off the land.
  • I will leave the Temple.
  • The Temple will become a heap and a disgrace.

The king knew it was his responsibility to build the House of the Lord. Therefore, he gathered a work force, brought cedar wood from Lebanon, and had men quarry the large stones for the foundation. He began building the Temple 480 years after Israel came out of Egypt, and the entire construction took seven years.

There were no sounds of tools at the Temple site because everything was shaped away from the project. Once it was done, the inside walls were totally covered with cedar. The inner sanctuary was covered with pure gold.

King Solomon assembled all the leaders from each tribe of Israel, and the Ark of God was moved into the Most Holy Place. Suddenly, the Glory of the Lord filled the Temple like a cloud. God's presence was so awesome that the priests could not fulfill their duties. The king faced the people and blessed them, and then he gave a prayer of dedication to the Lord. When all was done, the people praised the Lord and returned to their homes.

God met with Solomon a second time and said, "I have sanctified the house you built for Me, and I will establish your kingdom forever if you will continue to walk with Me as your father did. But if you or your sons depart from Me, and disobey My commandments, I will take Israel off of this land, I will depart from this house, and it will become a heap and a disgrace."

Solomon ruled over Israel and became greater than all the kings on earth in riches and wisdom. The people lived in peace all the years that Solomon was king.

Telling the Story

SOLOMON

SOLOMON ASKS FOR WISDOM

Before David died, he made his son Solomon king of Israel. Solomon loved the Lord and tried to follow the example of his father. One day, the Lord appeared to him and asked, "What do you want Me to give you?"

Without hesitation, Solomon said, "Lord, my father was a great king, and I feel like a child who doesn't know anything. Yet, You have placed me over Your great people. If You will give me one thing, give me the understanding to rule them wisely."

The Lord was pleased with Solomon's answer. "You have asked for wisdom instead of long life, riches, or peace. Therefore I will give you wisdom like no one has ever had or ever will have. In addition I will also give you riches and honor. And – if you continue to follow Me like your father did – I will also give you long life."

SOLOMON USES WISDOM

Soon after this promise, two women came before Solomon with a complaint against each other. One said, "This woman and I live in the same house. I gave birth to a son, and three days later she gave birth to a son. While we were sleeping, she accidentally rolled over on her son and killed him. In the night, she took my child from beside me and put her dead son in his place. When I awoke in the morning to nurse my son, the child was dead. I then realized it was not my son at all, but hers. She has my child."

The other woman said, "No, the living child is mine and the dead one is hers!" The two began arguing in front of the king.

He turned to a guard and said, "Come here with a sword." Then pointing to the child, he said, "Divide the child in two and give each mother a half."

One woman cried out, "No, don't kill my son! She can have him! Please let him live."

The other woman said, "Yes, cut the child in half, so we both will have a part."

The king turned to the guard, "Give the child to the first woman. I know she is the mother because her heart cries out for the child."

When Israel heard this, they knew God had given wisdom to Solomon. He increased in wisdom over the years and wrote proverbs and songs. People came from other countries to hear him speak words of wisdom. God also gave Solomon great wealth.

SOLOMON BUILDS THE TEMPLE

The king knew it was his responsibility to build the House of the Lord. Therefore, he gathered a work force, brought cedar wood from Lebanon, and had men quarry the large stones for the foundation. He began building the Temple 480 years after Israel came out of Egypt, and the entire construction took seven years.

There were no sounds of tools at the Temple site because everything was shaped away from the project. Once it was done, the inside walls were totally covered with cedar. The inner sanctuary was covered with pure gold.

King Solomon assembled all the leaders from each tribe of Israel, and the Ark of God was moved into the Most Holy Place. Suddenly, the Glory of the Lord filled the Temple like a cloud. God's presence was so awesome that the priests could not fulfill their duties. The king faced the people and blessed them, and then he gave a prayer of dedication to the Lord. When all was done, the people praised the Lord and returned to their homes.

God met with Solomon a second time and said, "I have sanctified the house you built for Me, and I will establish your kingdom forever if you will continue to walk with Me as your father did. But if you or your sons depart from Me, and disobey My commandments, I will take Israel off of this land, I will depart from this house, and it will become a heap and a disgrace."

Solomon ruled over Israel and became greater than all the kings on earth in riches and wisdom. The people lived in peace all the years that Solomon was king.

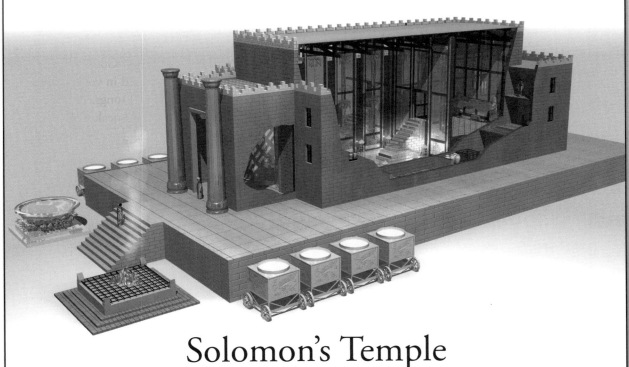

Solomon's Temple

- The crowning achievement of King Solomon's reign was the building of a magnificent Temple in about 960 B.C.

- When the Temple was completed, Solomon dedicated it with prayer and sacrifice, and even invited non-Jews to come and pray there.

- It functioned as a focal point of worship and sacrifices for almost 400 years until it was destroyed by the Babylonians in 586 B.C.

Extra Storyboard

First
Cluster

Second
Cluster

Third
Cluster

Activities

Using the boxes below, give the storyboard in words or pictures.

First Cluster	Second Cluster	Third Cluster

Feel free to use blank pages to write down or draw additional clusters or ideas.

What did you learn about **God** from the story of *Solomon?*

_____

_____

_____

What did you learn about **people** from the story of *Solomon?*

_____

_____

_____

What was your **favorite** part of the story? Tell why.

_____

_____

_____

PROVERB: a pithy statement that helps you remember an important truth. Create a proverb based on this story.

_____

_____

BANNER OR BUMPER STICKER: Give the essence of this story in six words or less.

ACTIVITIES: Choose from the following, or create another activity that helps you learn the story.

Drama
- Act out the scene of King Solomon and the two mothers with their babies.

Illustrated Storytelling
- Study I Kings 5:1-18 and tell the story of how Solomon's house was built. Use a sample of cedar wood as a part of your presentation.

Group Activity
- Go to an open field and mark off an area of ground equal to the Temple measurements. (I Ki. 6:1-4)
- Game: Choose 12 quotes and happenings found in this story and write them on a piece of paper, leaving space in between to cut them apart. Make enough copies for several teams to participate and see who can get them in correct chronological order most quickly.

Music
- Find or create background music that expresses the moods of the different parts of this lesson – worship, suspense, music to work by, the majesty of the Temple, etc. Have a narrator read the story, accompanied by the appropriate background music.

Poetry
- Write a story-poem about Solomon.
- Perform a dramatic reading or recitation of a poem about Solomon's wisdom.

Craft
- Build a model of Solomon's Temple.

Research
- Research and present a report on a physical description of the Temple.
- Study and report on the Cedars of Lebanon. Tell why their wood was/is so valuable.
- Tell about other times when the Bible records that God filled a place with His Glory.
- Look in the book of Proverbs and make a list of Solomon's most famous wisdom sayings that are quoted in our world today.

Discussion
- If God were to offer you anything you wanted, what would you ask for?

TIE TO PREVIOUS STORY: Write how you would connect this story with the previous story.

_____

_____

_____

TELL THE STORY: To whom did you tell the story and what was their response?

_____

_____

_____

Quiz 30

Name _____

MULTIPLE CHOICE

Date _____

____ 1. God appeared to Solomon in _____ and said, " Ask what I shall give you."
      a. the Temple   b. a field   c. a dream

____ 2. Solomon asked for _____ to rule the Lord's people.
      a. wise counselors   b. a book of laws   c. an understanding heart

____ 3. God was _____ with Solomon's request.
      a. surprised   b. pleased   c. disappointed

____ 4. God said He would also give Solomon _____.
      a. mercy and truth   b. riches and honor   c. sons and daughters

____ 5. God said if Solomon would walk in the ways of the Lord, He would _____ his days.
      a. lengthen   b. shorten   c. brighten

____ 6. Two _____ came to King Solomon and told him their stories.
      a. men   b. women   c. servants

____ 7. They each had a _____, but one was dead and the other was alive.
      a. calf   b. lamb   c. child

____ 8. They both claimed the _____ one as their own.
      a. dead   b. living   c. bigger

____ 9. Solomon commanded that the baby be _____.
      a. divided   b. sold   c. given away

____ 10. All Israel saw that the _____ of God was in Solomon.
      a. face   b. wisdom   c. kindness

____ 11. His _____ spread throughout all the surrounding nations.
      a. fame   b. family   c. army

____ 12. Kings from other nations came to hear the _____ of Solomon.
      a. stories   b. wisdom   c. songs

____ 13. Solomon began to build the Temple _____ years after the Israelites came out of Egypt.
      a. 240   b. 360   c. 480

____ 14. The inside walls were made of _____ and the floors were made with cypress (fir).
      a. cedar   b. pine   c. oak

____ 15. The inner sanctuary was covered with pure _____.
      a. diamonds   b. onyx   c. gold

____ 16. Solomon's Temple took _____ years to build.
      a. three   b. seven   c. twelve

____ 17. The priests brought the _____ from the tabernacle and set it in the Most Holy Place.
      a. altar   b. Ark of God   c. incense

____ 18. When the priests came out of the Most Holy Place, _____ filled the house of the Lord.
      a. lightning   b. thunder   c. a cloud

____ 19. Solomon wrote 3,000 proverbs and more than 1,000 _____.
      a. songs   b. books   c. letters

____ 20. God warned that if His people forsook Him, He would remove Himself from the _____.
      a. Temple   b. city gate   c. city wall

(5 points each question)

SCORE _____

LESSON 31

KING OF ASSYRIA

CHOSEN CITY

JOHN WALSH

Search the Scriptures

Fill in the blanks

ISAIAH 36:1-10

1. When Hezekiah was king of Judah, _____, the king of _____ sent his army and invaded Judah.

2. The army commander (Rabshakeh) came to the city of _____ where he met outside the wall with several of King _____ officers.

3. He gave them a message for their king: "Who do you have your _____ in?"

4. "Pharaoh, king of _____ will be no help you."

5. "The _____ your God is the one who sent me to _____ you."

ISAIAH 36:11-22

6. Hezekiah's men replied, "Speak to us in the _____ language, because we understand it; don't speak in the _____ language because the people on the wall are listening."

7. Then Rabshakeh loudly proclaimed, "Don't let Hezekiah _____ you; he cannot _____ you from us. Don't listen if he says that the Lord will _____ you."

8. But King Hezekiah's people _____ because he had commanded them, "_____."

9. The men _____ their clothes and went back to King Hezekiah and told him _____.

ISAIAH 37:1-7

10. When King Hezekiah heard this he _____ his clothes, covered himself with _____, and went into _____.

11. He sent messengers to the prophet Isaiah and asked him to _____.

12. Isaiah told the men to tell King Hezekiah _____.

13. God said he would cause the Assyrian commander to return to _____ and fall by the sword in his own land.

ISAIAH 37:14-20

14. When Hezekiah received a _____ from the Assyrian King, he took it to _____ and spread it out before the _____.

15. Hezekiah wanted God to _____ and _____ all the words of Sennacherib that he sent to _____ the living God.

16. Assyria had destroyed many other nations and burned their _____ made of wood and stone.

17. Hezekiah prayed, "Oh, Lord, _____ so that all the kingdoms of the earth will know that _____."

ISAIAH 37:33-38

18. "I will defend this city to save it for _____ sake and for My servant _____ sake."

19. The angel of the Lord went to the _____ of the Assyrians and _____ 185,000 men.

20. Sennacherib returned to _____ where two of his sons came and _____ him.

Scripture Crossword

ISAIAH 36:1-22, ISAIAH 37:1-7, ISAIAH 37:14-20, ISAIAH 37:33-38

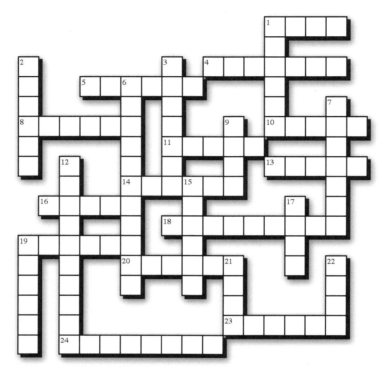

ACROSS

1 Isaiah was the son of ___.
4 King of Egypt
5 Hezekiah's people did not ___ the enemy's questions to them.
8 God made Rabshakeh ___ to his own land.
10 God saved Jerusalem for this man's sake.
11 The Lord said that Sennacherib would not "shoot an ___" into Jerusalem.
13 The ___ of the Lord killed 185,000 Assyrians.
14 Sennacherib destroyed many ___ of Judah.
16 Southern Kingdom
18 Hezekiah tore his clothes and put on ___.
19 Hezekiah received a ___ from Sennacherib.
20 Northern Kingdom
23 The Lord said about Jerusalem, "I will ___ this city!"
24 King of Judah

DOWN

1 Isaiah's message from the Lord to Hezekiah was, "Do not be ___."
2 Hezekiah's men begged their enemy, "Don't speak to us in ___!"
3 Hezekiah's request of Isaiah was for him to "pray for the ___."
6 King of Assyria
7 Sennacherib returned to ___.
9 Sennacherib's ___ killed him.
12 This story starts during the ___ year of Hezekiah's reign.
15 prophet who encouraged Hezekiah
17 God said He would put His ___ in the nose of Assyria.
19 Sennacherib's words were an insult to the ___ God.
21 The Assyrians claimed they were sent by the ___ to destroy Jerusalem.
22 Egypt: a broken (splintered) ___

Storyboard

Study the Storyboard until you can "see" the story

FIRST CLUSTER – Threats at the Wall

This story begins with a simple transition from Solomon to Hezekiah, which is over 200 years. It is a part of history that contains many wonderful stories.

Before you begin the story, picture the first scene of this crisis.
Envision a tent set up just outside the city wall. King Hezekiah's delegation is assembled under the tent and the commander of the Assyrian army is about to talk to them. Men are crowded on top of the wall, hoping to hear or see something.

The commander mocks the two hopes the people of Judah may be relying on – another nation coming to help, and the Lord helping. Remember these two hopes by pointing around you (another nation) and then up (the Lord).

The delegation is concerned about this man speaking in the Hebrew language and talking loud enough for those on the wall to hear. The commander laughs and talks louder. Remember this by cupping your hand behind your ear (the delegation), and both hands around your mouth as if you are yelling something (commander).

Now put it all together. Point around you, point up, cup your hand behind your ear, and both hands around your mouth as if yelling something. Repeat this several times until you can easily remember this part of the story.

> Your face portrays the life and emotions of the story.

After Solomon died, a civil war broke out, and the kingdom divided into two nations. The northern kingdom was called Israel, and the southern kingdom was called Judah.

The descendants of David ruled over Judah. Years later, Hezekiah became the king of Judah. He walked with God and honored Him. During his reign, the Assyrian empire conquered the northern kingdom of Israel and took the people totally off the land. Then the armies of Assyria moved south and invaded Judah.

Their commander arranged a conference outside the walls of Jerusalem, and Hezekiah sent a delegation to meet with him. The commander said, "Give this message to Hezekiah from Sennacherib, the great king of Assyria. Why are you so confident against my mighty army? Believe me, no other nation will come and help you. They all fear us."

"Oh, are you trusting in the Lord your God? Well, listen to me, it was your God who sent us here to destroy you!"

The Jewish delegation realized the commander was speaking loud enough so the people on the city wall could hear. They said, "Please, speak in your own language. We understand it."

The commander laughed and spoke louder, "No! This message is not only for your king. It is for the common men who stand on the wall. They are the ones who will suffer the most when we crush you."

He pointed to the men on the wall. "Listen to me! Don't trust your king or your God! Trust Sennacherib, the great king of Assyria! He will take good care of you. We have conquered many nations and their gods were not able to protect them. Your God cannot stop the great king of Assyria!"

GOD'S DELIVERANCE

The reactions to the commander are easy to remember, but here are a few hand gestures, which will help. Pretend to rip your clothes twice, put your hands together in prayer, and then give a message off to the side – rip, rip, prayer, message.

Once again cup your hand behind one ear ("I have heard"), and then cup your hand behind the other ear ("I will put a rumor into his ear"). End with a hand sign for murder (someone will murder him). Now put it all together:

rip, rip, prayer, message – ear, ear, murder

The delegation went back to Hezekiah and ripped their clothes in sorrow. When the king heard their report, he ripped his clothes as well. He went into the house of the Lord to pray, and sent messengers to the prophet Isaiah asking him to pray for God's people.

Isaiah sent word to Hezekiah. "The Lord says, 'I have heard this man's blaspheming! Do not be afraid. I will put a rumor into his ear and he will return to his own country. There, someone will murder him.'"

Suddenly, the commander heard of trouble in his land, and he knew the king of Assyria would need him. The entire army pulled up camp and returned to Nineveh, their capitol city.

SECOND CLUSTER – Threats by Letter

This whole section is a conversation between the King of Assyria and the Lord, but poor Hezekiah is caught in the middle! He is the one who receives the message from both sides.

The King's letter to God, through Hezekiah — None of the idols of the other nations have been able to resist him, why should God be any different? Hezekiah took the message to God and asked Him to do something about it.

God's answer to the King of Assyria through Hezekiah with a small note to Hezekiah — God's message to the King of Assyria divides into three parts:

(1) The king's worthlessness: *"Who do you think you are?*
    I have commanded Jerusalem to spit on you."

(2) The king's subordinate position: *"Who do you think you are mocking?*
    I am the Holy God of Israel. I am the one who put you in power
    so you would judge those other nations."

(3) The king's humiliation: *"Now you have become so arrogant that you rage against Me.*
    I am going to put a hook in your nose, a bit in your mouth,
    and take you back to the barn from which you came!"

You can remember these by pointing out, pointing in, and then making your finger into a hook. Pointing out is "Who do you think you are?" Pointing in is "Who do you think you're mocking?" Making a hook is "You have become so arrogant, I am going to put a hook in your nose …"

The nation of Judah was at peace for a time, until once again Sennacherib decided to move against

Jerusalem. He sent a message to Hezekiah. "Did your God tell you that you were safe from the king of Assyria? Don't believe Him! The other nations were not protected by their gods. I have conquered them all and burnt their gods with fire."

Hezekiah took the letter to the House of the Lord. He spread it out before God and prayed. "Oh Lord, look at this letter from the king of Assyria. He is saying You are like an idol made of wood or stone. Deliver us so all the nations of the earth will know You alone are God."

Isaiah sent a message to Hezekiah, which was God's answer to Sennacherib.

"Who do you think you are? I have commanded Jerusalem to spit on you. Who do you think you are mocking? I am the Holy God of Israel. I am the one who put you in power so you would judge those other nations. Now you have become so arrogant that you rage against Me. Therefore, I am going to put a hook in your nose, put a bit in your mouth, and take you back to the barn from which you came!"

"Hezekiah, don't worry about Sennacherib. Not one arrow will hit the walls of Jerusalem. Before his armies get here, they will turn around and go back to their country. I am your defense! I will save the city because of My promises to David."

GOD'S DELIVERANCE

I don't believe a storyboard is needed for this part of the story because it is so graphic. Just remember 185,000 soldiers died.

That evening the army of Assyria camped for the night. The sun went down and men sat around the campfire until it was time to sleep. When the sun arose the next morning, 185,000 solders were dead where they had slept. The great king of Assyria had an army of corpses!

He quickly returned home to Nineveh and knelt down before his idol. Two of his sons came in and killed him with a sword. Sennacherib, the great king of Assyria, was dead, and Jerusalem was at peace.

Assyrians

- During Isaiah's time, Assyria was the major world power, conquering one nation after another.
- The Assyrians practiced intense cruelty to their prisoners of war.
- Assyrian policy was to deport conquered peoples to other lands, thus destroying their sense of nationalism and making them lose attachment to their land. This made them more submissive to their conquerors.
- Nineveh was the capitol city of Assyria.

Telling the Story

THE KING OF ASSYRIA

THREATS AT THE WALL

After Solomon died, a civil war broke out, and the kingdom divided into two nations. The northern kingdom was called Israel, and the southern kingdom was called Judah.

The descendants of David ruled over Judah. Years later, Hezekiah became the king of Judah. He walked with God and honored Him. During his reign, the Assyrian empire conquered the northern kingdom of Israel and took the people totally off the land. Then the armies of Assyria moved south and invaded Judah.

Their commander arranged a conference outside the walls of Jerusalem, and Hezekiah sent a delegation to meet with him. The commander said, "Give this message to Hezekiah from Sennacherib, the great king of Assyria. Why are you so confident against my mighty army? Believe me, no other nation will come and help you. They all fear us."

"Oh, are you trusting in the Lord your God? Well, listen to me, it was your God who sent us here to destroy you!"

The Jewish delegation realized the commander was speaking loud enough so the people on the city wall could hear. They said, "Please, speak in your own language. We understand it."

The commander laughed and spoke louder, "No! This message is not only for your king. It is for the common men who stand on the wall. They are the ones who will suffer the most when we crush you."

He pointed to the men on the wall. "Listen to me! Don't trust your king or your God! Trust Sennacherib, the great king of Assyria! He will take good care of you. We have conquered many nations and their gods were not able to protect them. Your God cannot stop the great king of Assyria!"

The delegation went back to Hezekiah and ripped their clothes in sorrow. When the king heard their report, he ripped his clothes as well. He went into the house of the Lord to pray, and sent messengers to the prophet Isaiah asking him to pray for God's people.

Isaiah sent word to Hezekiah. "The Lord says, 'I have heard this man's blaspheming! Do not be afraid. I will put a rumor into his ear and he will return to his own country. There, someone will murder him.' "

Suddenly, the commander heard of trouble in his land, and he knew the king of Assyria would need him. The entire army pulled up camp and returned to Nineveh, their capitol city.

THREATS BY LETTER

The nation of Judah was at peace for a time, until once again Sennacherib decided to move against Jerusalem. He sent a message to Hezekiah. "Did your God tell you that you were safe from the king of Assyria? Don't believe Him! The other nations were not protected by their gods. I have conquered them all and burnt their gods with fire."

Hezekiah took the letter to the House of the Lord. He spread it out before God and prayed. "Oh Lord, look at this letter from the king of Assyria. He is saying You are like an idol made of wood or stone. Deliver us so all the nations of the earth will know You alone are God."

Isaiah sent a message to Hezekiah, which was God's answer to Sennacherib.

"Who do you think you are? I have commanded Jerusalem to spit on you. Who do you think you are mocking? I am the Holy God of Israel. I am the one who put you in power so you would judge those other nations. Now you have become so arrogant that you rage against Me. Therefore, I am going to put a hook in your nose, put a bit in your mouth, and take you back to the barn from which you came!"

"Hezekiah, don't worry about Sennacherib. Not one arrow will hit the walls of Jerusalem. Before his armies get here, they will turn around and go back to their country. I am your defense! I will save the city because of My promises to David."

That evening the army of Assyria camped for the night. The sun went down and men sat around the campfire until it was time to sleep. When the sun arose the next morning, 185,000 solders were dead where they had slept. The great king of Assyria had an army of corpses! He quickly returned home to Nineveh and knelt down before his idol. Two of his sons came in and killed him with a sword. Sennacherib, the great king of Assyria, was dead, and Jerusalem was at peace.

The Divided Kingdom

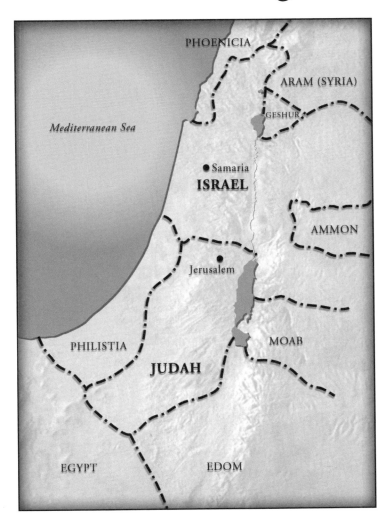

Extra Storyboard

Second
Cluster

First
Cluster

Activities

Using the boxes below, give the storyboard in words or pictures.

First Cluster	Second Cluster

Feel free to use blank pages to write down or draw additional clusters or ideas.

What did you learn about **God** from the story of *The King of Assyria?*

_____

_____

_____

What did you learn about **people** from the story of *The King of Assyria?*

_____

_____

_____

What was your **favorite** part of the story? Tell why.

_____

_____

_____

PROVERB: a pithy statement that helps you remember an important truth. Create a proverb based on this story.

_____

_____

BANNER OR BUMPER STICKER: Give the essence of this story in six words or less.

ACTIVITIES: Choose from the following, or create another activity that helps you learn the story.

Drama
- Have a narrator read the story while actors pantomime the actions taking place.

Storytelling
- Use puppets to tell this story. Include conversations between (1) the Assyrian army commander and Hezekiah's men, (2) Hezekiah's men and King Hezekiah (3) Hezekiah's men and Isaiah (4) Isaiah and Hezekiah.
- "You Are There" A news reporter on the scene is telling what he sees and hears. There may be some noise in the background. Occasionally, he pulls someone aside from the crowd and asks him/her questions about what is happening.

Group Activity
- Charades: Silently portray the actions of various characters in the story. Some of these characters might include Rabshakeh (the Assyrian army commander), some of Hezekiah's representatives, men on the wall, King Hezekiah, messengers, Isaiah, angel of the Lord, Sennacherib, and sons of Sennacherib.

Poetry
- Do a dramatic presentation of *The Destruction of Sennacherib*, by Lord Byron.
- Write a poem of your own about this event.

Research
- Study the Divided Kingdom and where the various tribes of Israel were located.
- What are the different possibilities of what happened to the northern 10 tribes?
- What was the significance of "renting" (tearing) one's clothes to express sorrow in Biblical times?
- What did the god Baal require of his worshippers?

Writing
- Find what is recorded in secular history about Sennacherib and give a report on your findings.
- Report on the Assyrian Empire.

TIE TO PREVIOUS STORY: Write how you would connect this story with the previous story.

_____

_____

_____

TELL THE STORY: To whom did you tell the story and what was their response?

_____

_____

_____

Quiz 31

Name _____

Date _____

MATCHING

___ 1. Pharaoh   a. King of Assyria

___ 2. Isaiah   b. King of Judah

___ 3. Sennacherib   c. King of Egypt

___ 4. Hezekiah   d. Assyrian army commander

___ 5. Rabshakeh   e. prophet of God

MULTIPLE CHOICE

___ 6. The Assyrian army commander spoke with a delegation of Hezekiah's men _____.
    a. outside the wall   b. at the temple   c. inside the city gate

___ 7. Rabshakeh told Hezekiah's men, "_____ told me to destroy you."
    a. my king   b. your priest   c. the Lord

___ 8. The Jewish men didn't want the _____ to hear such words.
    a. children who were playing   b. women drawing water   c. people on the wall

___ 9. After that, Rabshakeh spoke _____.
    a. very quietly   b. very loudly   c. in a different language

___ 10. He told the people not to _____ Hezekiah.
    a. hurt   b. believe   c. resist

___ 11. According to their king's command, the men of Jerusalem said _____.
    a. nothing   b. "God is great!"   c. "Return to your country."

___ 12. When Hezekiah heard all this, he tore his clothes, covered himself in sackcloth, and went to the ___.
    a. city gate   b. town square   c. House of the Lord

___ 13. He sent a message to the prophet Isaiah asking him to _____.
    a. come and visit   b. pray for them   c. speak to the Assyrians

___ 14. Isaiah sent a message back saying "Don't be _____."
    a. afraid   b. deceived   c. proud

___ 15. God caused the army commander to hear a rumor and _____ his own land.
    a. destroy   b. flee from   c. return to

___ 16. Hezekiah received a letter from the king of _____.
    a. Assyria   b. Babylon   c. Egypt

___ 17. The words of Sennacherib showed _____ for the living God.
    a. respect   b. disrespect   c. fear

___ 18. Hezekiah wanted God to protect Jerusalem so all the world would know that _____.
    a. Assyria was wicked   b. God's people were faithful   c. He alone was God

___ 19. God said He would defend Jerusalem for His own sake and for His servant _____ sake.
    a. Hezekiah's   b. David's   c. Isaiah's

___ 20. Sennacherib was killed by two of _____.
    a. his sons   b. Hezekiah's men   c. God's angels

(5 points each question)   SCORE _____

LESSON 32

KING HEZEKIAH

CHOSEN CITY

JOHN WALSH

Search the Scriptures

Fill in the blanks

ISAIAH 38:1-22

1. King Hezekiah was _____.

2. The prophet Isaiah told the king to _____

   because _____.

3. Then Hezekiah _____ and prayed.

4. He asked God to remember _____.

5. Then the king _____.

6. God gave Isaiah another message for the king: "I have heard your _____ and

   I have seen your _____.

7. I will add to your life _____."

8. The sign that the Lord gave to Hezekiah was that the sun would _____.

ISAIAH 39:1-8

9. When the son of the king of _____ heard of King Hezekiah's illness and recovery,

   he sent _____ to Hezekiah.

10. Hezekiah showed his visitors _____.

11. List the various things he showed them: _____

    _____

12. Isaiah the prophet came and asked king Hezekiah, "What did these men say and

    _____?"

13. Hezekiah answered, "They came to me from _____."

14. Isaiah asked, " What have they _____ in your house?"

15. The king answered, "They have seen _____ that is in my house."

16. "There is _____ among my _____ that I have not shown them."

17. Isaiah told King Hezekiah that the days would come that _____ in his house would

    be _____ to Babylon and _____ would be left.

18. Even some of Hezekiah's descendants would be taken to the _____ of the king of Babylon.

19. Hezekiah said, "The word of the Lord that you have spoken is _____."

20. "At least there will be _____ in my days."

Scripture Crossword

ISAIAH 38:1-22, ISAIAH 39:1-8

ACROSS

3 Hezekiah showed his visitors ___ in his palace.
6 Hezekiah received ___ and a gift from Babylon.
7 God's sign to Hezekiah was that he would move the ___ backwards.
8 Hezekiah was glad there would be ___ during his lifetime.
10 Hezekiah's visitors saw his silver and ___.
12 one of Hezekiah's ancestors
13 Hezekiah was told to put his house in ___.
16 Hezekiah was told he was going to ___.
19 Hezekiah's visitors came from ___.
20 God gave Hezekiah a ___ that he would be healed.
21 Hezekiah turned to the wall and ___.
22 timekeeping instrument

DOWN

1 Hezekiah ___ bitterly.
2 God said, "I have seen your ___."
4 Hezekiah went to the ___ of the Lord and gave thanks.
5 king whose life was extended by God
7 Hezekiah's condition
8 Some of Hezekiah's descendants would become servants in the ___ of the king of Babylon.
9 God added ___ years to Hezekiah's life.
10 Hezekiah said, "The word of the Lord is ___."
11 God said, "I have heard your ___."
14 God said, "I will ___ this city."
15 ___ were laid on Hezekiah's boil.
17 prophet who spoke God's words to Hezekiah
18 king of Babylon

Storyboard

Study the Storyboard until you can "see" the story

FIRST CLUSTER – Answered Prayer

You can remember this cluster by pointing both hands down, putting them together in prayer, and then pointing them up.
- Point down – "You're going to die."
- Together in prayer – Hezekiah praying and crying
- Pointing up – Hezekiah looks up and sees the sun move back 10°.

King Hezekiah became seriously ill. The prophet Isaiah came to him and said, "God has told me you will not live through this illness. So prepare to die."

After Isaiah left the room, Hezekiah cried out to the Lord. "Oh God! I have walked with You and lived according to Your commandments. Please spare my life." He then turned his head to the wall and cried bitterly.

Once again, God talked to Isaiah. "Go tell King Hezekiah I have heard his prayer and have seen his tears. Therefore I will add fifteen years to his life. I will also give him assurance by verifying this promise. Tell him to watch the shadow on the sundial. I will cause it to go backward ten degrees."

So it happened. As Hezekiah watched, the shadow on the sundial moved backward ten degrees. Immediately his illness started to improve and he totally recovered. He sang before the Lord and gave thanks.

SECOND CLUSTER – Showing Off

This cluster involves the king and a delegation from Babylon. What happens is fairly easy to retell, but there is a list to remember – the various valuable things he showed the delegation.

Imagine a gold plate with a wide rim of silver. A small mound of spices is on the plate with oil poured on top. The plate is sitting next to a pile of treasure. Review this mental picture until you can easily give the list of valuable items Hezekiah showed the delegation. (gold, silver, spices, oil, and treasure)

After his recovery, a delegation came from Babylon and presented him with letters and gifts. They stated that the king of Babylon wished him well and expressed thankfulness, having heard about his illness and recovery.

Hezekiah was pleased with this expression of kindness. He honored the delegation with a tour of his palace and government buildings. He took them to the treasury house and showed them all of the gold, silver, spices, precious oil, and valuable treasures. He showed them everything of value.

THIRD CLUSTER – The Future

This cluster is a conversation between the king and Isaiah. Use your hands to help remember what they said. Point in, out, in, out, in, out. "In" points toward Isaiah and "out" points toward King Hezekiah. The conversation goes like this: (in) *Who were those men?* (out) *They were from a far-off country.* (in) *What did you show them?* (out) *Everything!* (in) *They will come and take everything.* (out) *That's good!*

After the men from Babylon left, the prophet Isaiah came in to visit the king. He asked, "Who were those men and what did they say to you?"

"They were from a far-off country – a place called Babylon."

"What did you show them?"

"I showed them everything. I did not hide anything of value from them."

Isaiah paused and then said, "Listen to the words of the Lord. 'A day will come when Babylon will invade Judah and take everything you have shown them back to their country. Your descendants will become personal slaves to the king of Babylon.' "

Hezekiah looked at Isaiah, and finally said, "This message from the Lord is good. None of this will happen during my lifetime. While I live, there will be peace and security." So Hezekiah now knew the fate of Judah, and he was content.

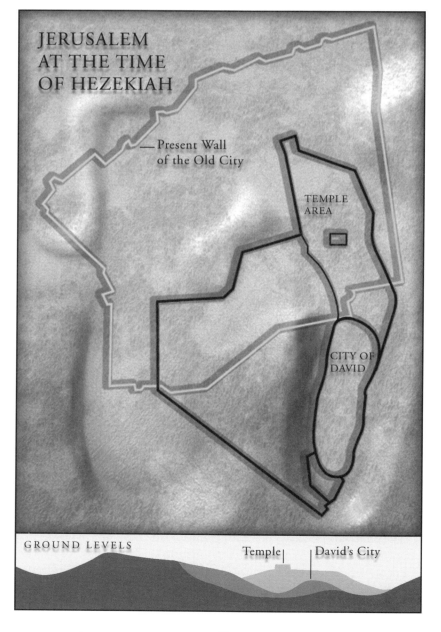

Telling the Story

KING HEZEKIAH

King Hezekiah became seriously ill. The prophet Isaiah came to him and said, "God has told me you will not live through this illness. So prepare to die."

After Isaiah left the room, Hezekiah cried out to the Lord. "Oh God! I have walked with You and lived according to Your commandments. Please spare my life." He then turned his head to the wall and cried bitterly.

Once again, God talked to Isaiah. "Go tell King Hezekiah I have heard his prayer and have seen his tears. Therefore I will add fifteen years to his life. I will also give him assurance by verifying this promise. Tell him to watch the shadow on the sundial. I will cause it to go backward ten degrees."

So it happened. As Hezekiah watched, the shadow on the sundial moved backward ten degrees. Immediately his illness started to improve and he totally recovered. He sang before the Lord and gave thanks.

After his recovery, a delegation came from Babylon and presented him with letters and gifts. They stated that the king of Babylon wished him well and expressed thankfulness, having heard about his illness and recovery.

Hezekiah was pleased with this expression of kindness.

He honored the delegation with a tour of his palace and government buildings.

He took them to the treasury house and showed them all of the gold, silver, spices, precious oil, and valuable treasures. He showed them everything of value. After the men from Babylon left, the prophet Isaiah came in to visit the king. He asked, "Who were those men and what did they say to you?"

"They were from a far-off country – a place called Babylon."

"What did you show them?"

"I showed them everything. I did not hide anything of value from them."

Isaiah paused and then said, "Listen to the words of the Lord. 'A day will come when Babylon will invade Judah and take everything you have shown them back to their country. Your descendants will become personal slaves to the king of Babylon.' "

Hezekiah looked at Isaiah, and finally said, "This message from the Lord is good. None of this will happen during my lifetime. While I live, there will be peace and security." So Hezekiah now knew the fate of Judah, and he was content.

Extra Storyboard

First
Cluster

Second
Cluster

Third
Cluster

Activities

Using the boxes below, give the storyboard in words or pictures.

First Cluster	Second Cluster	Third Cluster

Feel free to use blank pages to write down or draw additional clusters or ideas.

What did you learn about **God** from the story of *King Hezekiah?*

_____

_____

_____

What did you learn about **people** from the story of *King Hezekiah?*

_____

_____

_____

What was your **favorite** part of the story? Tell why.

_____

_____

_____

PROVERB: a pithy statement that helps you remember an important truth. Create a proverb based on this story.

_____

_____

BANNER OR BUMPER STICKER: Give the essence of this story in six words or less.

ACTIVITIES: Choose from the following, or create another activity that helps you learn the story.

Drama

- Act out this story in a modern way. Possibly the prophet Isaiah is making a bedside visit to the sick king. Isaiah delivers God's messages to Hezekiah by reaching in his briefcase and pulling out a notepad from which he reads the words of God. God's message might also be pre-recorded on a CD and then played for the king.
- Have a bystander or a servant tell the story from his point of view.

Dramatic Monologue

- Tell the story in the first-person as if you were King Hezekiah.

Storytelling

- Use puppets to tell this story.

Art

- Create a set of colored pictures to use as illustrations for telling this story in front of a group.

Craft

- Make a sundial. Show how it works and why it would be a miracle for the shadow to go backward.

Research

- What do we know about King Hezekiah's life before the beginning of this story?
- What important events happened in the extra 15 years added to Hezekiah's life? It is important to mention his son Manasseh and what he was known for. II Chronicles 33
- Explain the value of a "poultice of figs" that the prophet said to use on King Hezekiah for his healing.
- What were the world powers during Hezekiah's life and what events happened soon after his death?

Discussion

- Find other examples of when God seems to change His plan of action in response to the prayer of one of His children.
- Kings often showed off the treasures of their kingdom. Solomon did it. Why was it so crucial when Hezekiah did it?
- What would you do if God told you that you would live for 15 more years?

TIE TO PREVIOUS STORY: Write how you would connect this story with the previous story.

_____

_____

_____

TELL THE STORY: To whom did you tell the story and what was their response?

_____

_____

_____

Quiz 32

Name _____

Date _____

MATCHING - Messages

____ 1. Isaiah's first message to Hezekiah

____ 2. Isaiah's second message to Hezekiah

____ 3. Isaiah's third message to Hezekiah

a. your descendants will be taken away

b. prepare for imminent death

c. God has heard and answered your prayer

MATCHING

____ 4. God

____ 5. sun

____ 6. Isaiah

____ 7. son of the king of Babylon

____ 8. 15 years

____ 9. 10 degrees (steps)

____ 10. Babylon

____ 11. the word of the Lord

d. how much the sundial went backward

e. far away country

f. happy to hear of Hezekiah's recovery

g. extended Hezekiah's life

h. went backward

i. was added to Hezekiah's life

j. Hezekiah declared it "good"

k. delivered God's messages

MATCHING - Hezekiah

____ 12. Hezekiah

____ 13. Hezekiah's descendants

____ 14. Hezekiah's visitors

____ 15. Hezekiah's illness

____ 16. Hezekiah's prayer

____ 17. Hezekiah's tears

____ 18. Hezekiah's treasures

____ 19. Hezekiah's days (reign)

____ 20. Hezekiah's death

l. seen by Babylonians

m. brought letters and gifts

n. turned to the wall and wept

o. heard by God (a plea for life)

p. seen by God

q. threatened to kill him

r. filled with peace

s. delayed for years

t. some would be taken to Babylonian king's palace

(5 points each question)

SCORE _____

LESSON 33

JEREMIAH

CHOSEN CITY

JOHN WALSH

Search the Scriptures

Fill in the blanks

JEREMIAH 1:1-9

1. In the days when Josiah, Jehoiakim, and Zedekiah were kings of Judah, the word of the Lord came to _____, the prophet.

2. The Lord said that the prophet should _____ wherever God would send him and _____ the words He commanded him. The Lord said, "I have put My _____ in your mouth."

JEREMIAH 19:1-15

3. The Lord told Jeremiah to take a _____ and go speak to the people in the city of _____.

4. What did the Lord say He was going to do to that place?_____

5. Because the people had forsaken God, what was going to happen to them?_____
_____

6. Then Jeremiah was to _____ in the sight of all the men, and tell them that _____ would do the same to Jerusalem and its inhabitants.

JEREMIAH 20:1-9

7. After Jeremiah delivered his message, he was _____ and put in _____ by Pashur, the priest who was in charge of the house of the Lord.

8. The next morning, Jeremiah told Pashur that from that time on he would be called by a name that meant "_____."

9. God said He would give all of Judah into the hand of the king of _____.

10. The king would take away some of the people as _____, and some would be _____.

11. Jeremiah said that even _____ himself would be taken captive into Babylon where he would _____.

12. When Jeremiah thought about not speaking any more in God's name, God's word was in his heart as a _____ shut up in his bones, and he could not keep quiet.

JEREMIAH 21: 3-7

13. God told Jeremiah to tell his people, "_____ will fight against you…
in _____, and fury…I will strike down the inhabitants of this city – both _____ and _____ – with a great plague. Any who survive I will give over into the hand of
_____, king of Babylon, and he will strike them down with the
_____."

II KINGS 24:1-6

14. When Jehoiakim was king of Judah, he came under the authority of King _____.

15. Then Jehoiakim _____, he was taken captive, and his _____ became king in his place.

II KINGS 24:10-15

16. When Jehoiachin was king of Judah, Nebuchadnezzar's army besieged Jerusalem and took the king captive along with _____.

17. The Babylonians also carried out all the _____ of the House of the Lord, and all of the treasures of the king's _____, and cut in pieces all the vessels of _____ that Solomon had made in the Temple of the Lord.

18. The Babylonians took _____ captives, leaving only the _____ people of the land.

II KINGS 24:18-20, 25:8-10

19. The next king of Judah was _____, who also did _____ in the sight of the Lord and who also _____ against the king of Babylon.

20. The Babylonians came to Jerusalem where they burned the House of the _____, the king's _____, and all the houses of Jerusalem. They also broke down the _____ around Jerusalem.

JEREMIAH 23:5-6

21. The Lord declared that in the future He will raise up for David a _____ who will reign as king and bring justice and judgment in the earth. The name by which He will be called is _____.

JEREMIAH 24:1-10

22. The Lord showed Jeremiah two baskets of _____ sitting in front of the Temple.

23. One basket had _____, and the other basket had _____ _____.

24. God said the good figs made him think of those people whom He sent away captive to a foreign land; He would keep his _____ on them and bring them back again to their land and _____ them there.

25. God said they would be his _____ and He would be their _____, and they would _____ to Him with _____.

26. The _____ figs symbolized those people who _____ in their land at first, but who were later carried away and destroyed.

JEREMIAH 29:10-14

27. The Lord promised that after _____ years in Babylon, His people would be brought back to their own land.

28. God says, "You will seek Me and find Me when you _____ Me with all your _____.

29. God promised to bring His people back from all the _____ and all the places where He sent them into exile.

Teaching with an Object Lesson

The prophet Jeremiah carried a clay pot and stood before the leaders and priests of Judah. They looked at the clay pot and then looked at the prophet.

Jeremiah said, "The people of Judah have forsaken the Lord and have decided to worship idols of their own making. Therefore, I have a message from the Lord!"

He then threw the clay pot onto the stone floor and it broke into pieces!

"The Lord says, 'Because my people have turned away from Me, I am going to cause them to be slaughtered by their enemies. I will totally destroy the city of Jerusalem and make it a complete disgrace in the eyes of everyone who looks upon it.

It will lie in ruins just like this clay pot!' "

Scripture Crossword

Jer.1:1-9, Jer.19:1-15, Jer.20:1-9, Jer.21: 3-7, Jer.23: 5-6. Jer.24:1-10, Jer.29:10-14
II Kings 24:1-20, II Kings 25:8-10

ACROSS

1 "The Lord Our ___"
5 Jehoiachin's ___ was taken captive with him.
6 The last king Jeremiah prophesied to
8 The captivity was to last for ___ years.
9 Good figs: captives from ___
13 God told Jeremiah to ___ the clay pot.
14 Jehoiakim ___ against Nebuchadnezzar.
17 God said the captives would ___ to Him with their whole hearts.
19 The Lord showed Jeremiah two baskets of ___.
20 Pashur had Jeremiah ___.
22 The Babylonian army broke down the ___ of Jerusalem.
24 King when Jeremiah first became prophet
25 God knew Jeremiah before he was ___.
27 God said the people's carcasses would feed the birds and the ___.
28 God told Jeremiah to buy a jar from a ___.

DOWN

2 God said, "I will ___ you from all the nations."
3 Zedekiah was how old when he became king?
4 "You will ___ me and find me when you search with all your heart."
7 God promised to give the captives a ___ to know Him.
10 Zedekiah did ___ in the sight of the Lord.
11 Pashur's new name meant what?
12 God told Jeremiah, "I have put ___ in your mouth."
13 The ___ figs could not be eaten.
15 Zedekiah rebelled against the king of ___.
16 Zedekiah reigned for ___ years.
18 Nebuchadnezzar took ___ from the temple.
19 Invaders set ___ to the temple and the palace.
21 The Lord promised to raise up a Righteous ___.
23 Jeremiah was put in ___.
26 One basket of figs was good and ___.

Storyboard

Study the Storyboard until you can "see" the story

FIRST CLUSTER – A Broken Clay Pot

Jeremiah used a clay pot to give the leaders of Judah a message from God. He destroyed the pot in front of them by throwing it on the floor. He then said God was about to fulfill an old promise He made to Solomon — leave the Temple, destroy Jerusalem, and take people off the land. Remember this by imagining the Temple with the city around it, and the people leaving the city.

The exchange between the prophet and priest was very dramatic and should be easy to remember. There is one list that needs to be remembered. The priest would experience three acts of terror – he would (1) see his friends die in the streets, (2) see the city destroyed and (3) die and be buried in a foreign country. (Friends, City, Foreign Country)

The prophet Jeremiah carried a clay pot and stood before the leaders and priests of Judah. They looked at the clay pot and then looked at the prophet. He said, "The people of Judah have forsaken the Lord and have decided to worship idols of their own making. Therefore, I have a message from the Lord!"

Jeremiah then threw the clay pot onto the stone floor and it broke into pieces! "The Lord says, 'Because my people have turned away from Me, I am going to cause them to be slaughtered by their enemies. I will totally destroy the city of Jerusalem and make it a complete disgrace in the eyes of everyone who looks upon it. It will lie in ruins just like this clay pot.' "

One of the priests became so angry, he had Jeremiah beaten, put in stocks, and left to suffer. The next day the priest came and released him. Jeremiah looked at him and said, "The Lord has changed your name. It is now 'Terror.' You will be in terror the rest of your life. In terror you will see your friends killed in the streets. In terror you will watch the armies of Babylon destroy this city. Still, you will live and be taken captive back to Babylon. There you will die; and there you will be buried."

SECOND CLUSTER – The King of Babylon Comes to Judah

Nebuchadnezzar went to Jerusalem three times. Each time Jeremiah warned the people to cooperate, but they refused. Babylon destroyed more of the city with each visit, until it was in total ruins. Remember the uniqueness of each visit by thinking "prophecy," "treasures," and "God's fight."

1st visit — Jeremiah told the people the Captivity would last for 70 years.
2nd visit — Babylon took the Temple treasures, and 10,000 of the best people.
3rd visit — God told the rulers He was the one fighting against them.

Jeremiah continued to tell the people they would be taken away from their homeland. He said, "You will be in captivity for seventy years, then God will bring your children back to this land." Still, the people refused to listen to him.

Finally Nebuchadnezzar, the king of Babylon, came to do battle with Judah. Nebuchadnezzar conquered Jerusalem and took Judah's king back to Babylon where he died. His son was made king in his place.

Jeremiah told the people to accept this and submit to Babylon. Again, they did not listen, but rebelled against Nebuchadnezzar. So the armies of Babylon came and conquered the city a second time. They took the king and his family back to Babylon, along with all the treasures and gold from the House of the Lord. They took everything of value from the city, including all the craftsmen, military men, and scholars. Ten thousand people were marched off to Babylon, leaving only the poor to oversee the land.

Again the people rebelled against Babylon, so Nebuchadnezzar sent his army to Judah a third time. The rulers of Jerusalem sent a message to Jeremiah. "Please, pray and ask God to deliver us!"

The Lord sent a message back to them through Jeremiah, "No! I will not deliver you. I am the one fighting against you. I will strike you down with a great plague, and give those who survive to Nebuchadnezzar."

Still, the people ignored this warning. Therefore Nebuchadnezzar decided to leave no one in Judah who could resist him. When the army of Babylon conquered the city, they destroyed the Temple, burned all the houses, and broke down the city walls. They took the rest of the people away to Babylon, leaving only a few to tend the land.

THIRD CLUSTER – Two Baskets of Figs

The Lord showed Jeremiah two baskets of figs. When Jeremiah looked at them, he saw the future of Israel during the time of captivity. This story provides its own storyboard, but the main thing to remember is God's five promises for those in captivity:

1. I am going to watch over My people and care for them.
2. I will bring their descendants back into this land and once again plant them here.
3. I will put a desire into their heart to know Me.
4. I will be their God and they shall be My people.
5. I will give them a Righteous Branch, "The Lord our Righteousness"

I visualize it this way:
- God is caring for a potted fig plant.
- He takes it back to where it came from, and plants it.
- The plant looks up at God in love.
- God says, "I am yours, and you are Mine!"
- Suddenly a special branch grows out of the plant.

The Lord came to Jeremiah in a vision. He showed him two baskets of figs and asked, "What do you see?"

Jeremiah looked at them and said, "I see two baskets of figs. One is full of delicious fruit, the best I have seen. It makes my mouth water just looking at it. The other contains rotten figs, the worst I have seen. The smell is repulsive."

The Lord said, "The people who stay here in Judah are like the rotten figs. They are evil and corrupt. I will throw them away and have them destroyed."

"The people taken away into the captivity are like the good figs. I am going to watch over them and care for them. I will bring their descendants back into this land and once again plant them here. I will put a desire into their hearts to know Me. I will be their God and they shall be My people.

I shall raise up a righteous Branch from the line of David, and He will bring justice and righteousness to the land. He will be called, 'The Lord our Righteousness.' "

The vision about the rotten figs was fulfilled when the people in Judah once again rebelled against Babylon. They killed the governor appointed by Nebuchadnezzar, and then in fear they fled to Egypt. Meanwhile, the Lord was with those who were taken to Babylon, and He sent His prophets to be with them

Telling the Story

JEREMIAH

A BROKEN CLAY POT

The prophet Jeremiah carried a clay pot and stood before the leaders and priests of Judah. They looked at the clay pot and then looked at the prophet. He said, "The people of Judah have forsaken the Lord and have decided to worship idols of their own making. Therefore, I have a message from the Lord!"

Jeremiah then threw the clay pot onto the stone floor and it broke into pieces! "The Lord says, 'Because my people have turned away from Me, I am going to cause them to be slaughtered by their enemies. I will totally destroy the city of Jerusalem and make it a complete disgrace in the eyes of everyone who looks upon it. It will lie in ruins just like this clay pot.' "

One of the priests became so angry, he had Jeremiah beaten, put in stocks, and left to suffer. The next day the priest came and released him. Jeremiah looked at him and said, "The Lord has changed your name. It is now 'Terror.' You will be in terror the rest of your life. In terror you will see your friends killed in the streets. In terror you will watch the armies of Babylon destroy this city. Still, you will live and be taken captive back to Babylon. There you will die; and there you will be buried."

THE KING OF BABYLON COMES TO JUDAH

Jeremiah continued to tell the people they would be taken away from their homeland. He said, "You will be in captivity for seventy years, then God will bring your children back to this land." Still, the people refused to listen to him.

Finally Nebuchadnezzar, the king of Babylon, came to do battle with Judah. Nebuchadnezzar conquered Jerusalem and took Judah's king back to Babylon where he died. His son was made king in his place.

Jeremiah told the people to accept this and submit to Babylon. Again, they did not listen, but rebelled against Nebuchadnezzar. So the armies of Babylon came and conquered the city a second time. They took the king and his family back to Babylon, along with all the treasures and gold from the House of the Lord. They took everything of value from the city, including all the craftsmen, military men, and scholars. Ten thousand people were marched off to Babylon, leaving only the poor to oversee the land.

Again the people rebelled against Babylon, so Nebuchadnezzar sent his army to Judah a third time. The rulers of Jerusalem sent a message to Jeremiah. "Please, pray and ask God to deliver us!"

The Lord sent a message back to them through Jeremiah, "No! I will not deliver you. I am the one fighting against you. I will strike you down with a great plague, and give those who survive to Nebuchadnezzar."

Again, the people ignored this warning. Therefore Nebuchadnezzar decided to leave no one in Judah who could resist him. When the army of Babylon conquered the city, they destroyed the Temple, burned all the houses, and broke down the city walls. They took the rest of the people away to Babylon, leaving only a few to tend the land.

TWO BASKETS OF FIGS

The Lord came to Jeremiah in a vision. He showed him two baskets of figs and asked, "What do you see?"

Jeremiah looked at them and said, "I see two baskets of figs. One is full of delicious fruit, the best I have seen. It makes my mouth water just looking at it. The other contains rotten figs, the worst I have seen. The smell is repulsive."

The Lord said, "The people who stay here in Judah are like the rotten figs. They are evil and corrupt. I will throw them away and have them destroyed."

"The people taken away into the captivity are like the good figs. I am going to watch over them and care for them. I will bring their descendants back into this land and once again plant them here. I will put a desire into their hearts to know Me. I will be their God and they shall be My people.

I shall raise up a righteous Branch from the line of David, and He will bring justice and righteousness to the land. He will be called, 'The Lord our Righteousness.' "

The vision about the rotten figs was fulfilled when the people in Judah once again rebelled against Babylon. They killed the governor appointed by Nebuchadnezzar, and then in fear they fled to Egypt. Meanwhile, the Lord was with those who were taken to Babylon, and He sent His prophets to be with them.

Figs

- Figs are cherished by some in ancient times as a symbol of peace and prosperity
- There are at least 600 known varieties of figs
- Figs are a delicate, plump, tear-drop shaped fruit the size of a medium plum
- Figs are best eaten when very soft. They are also highly perishable

Activities

Using the boxes below, give the storyboard in words or pictures.

First Cluster	Second Cluster	Third Cluster

Feel free to use blank pages to write down or draw additional clusters or ideas.

What did you learn about **God** from the story of *Jeremiah*?

_____

_____

_____

What did you learn about **people** from the story of *Jeremiah*?

_____

_____

_____

What was your **favorite** part of the story? Tell why.

_____

_____

_____

PROVERB: a pithy statement that helps you remember an important truth. Create a proverb based on this story.

_____

_____

BANNER OR BUMPER STICKER: Give the essence of this story in six words or less.

ACTIVITIES: Choose from the following, or create another activity that helps you learn the story.

Drama
- Act out the first part of this story, including the response Jeremiah received from the people to whom he was speaking.

Dramatic Monologue
- Act as if you are the prophet Jeremiah. Deliver God's message, and then smash a clay pot to illustrate what you are saying.

Illustrated Storytelling
- Object Lesson: Tell the story using at least five different objects to illustrate it.
- Prepare two baskets of figs – good and bad. Give the speech God gave Jeremiah about the figs. Have participants taste the good figs, and smell the bad ones before throwing them away.
- Food: Bring in as many samples of figs as possible. These could be fresh, dried, baked, or in preserves.

Art
- Draw a series of pictures to show the events of this story in the order they took place.

Writing
- Write a descriptive newspaper article about what happened in Israel during this time in its history.

Research
- Study the importance of names. Find all the times in the Bible when God changed someone's name and tell the significance of it.
- Contrast the way Jehoiachin was treated by the Babylonians with the way Zedekiah was treated. Report on the difference and what might account for it. II Kings 24 & 25, II Chronicles 36:11-21, Jeremiah 52:31-34

Discussion
- Why was God angry with His people?
- Describe the behavior that Jeremiah told God's people to have while they were in captivity. Jeremiah 29:1-7
- Discuss the various ways that things are preserved by putting them in captivity – people, fruit preserves sealed in jars, scrolls sealed in the cave of Qumram, etc.
- What did Jeremiah mean when he spoke of the "Righteous Branch" in David's line?

TIE TO PREVIOUS STORY: Write how you would connect this story with the previous story.

_____

_____

_____

TELL THE STORY: To whom did you tell the story and what was their response?

_____

_____

_____

Quiz 33

Name _____

Date _____

MATCHING

___ 1. Jeremiah

___ 2. basket of bad figs

___ 3. Jewish captives in other lands

___ 4. basket of good figs

___ 5. poorest people

___ 6. vessels of gold

___ 7. treasures of the Lord's House

___ 8. Zedekiah

___ 9. walls of Jerusalem

___ 10. The Lord

___ 11. words of the Lord

___ 12. potter's clay vessel

___ 13. Pashur

a. were carried away to Babylon

b. were cut in pieces

c. an evil king of Judah

d. were broken down by the Babylonians

e. God kept His eye on them

f. were left behind to care for the land

g. told Jeremiah what to say

h. like a burning fire in Jeremiah's bones

i. thrown down and broken in pieces by Jeremiah

j. had Jeremiah beaten and put in stocks

k. prophet during days of Josiah, Jehoiakim and Zedekiah

l. symbolized Israelites who were taken captive but later would be brought back to their own land by God

m. symbolized Israelites who remained in their land at first, and later were destroyed by famine, pestilence, and the sword

MULTIPLE CHOICE

___ 14. When God's people turned away from Him, God _____ Jerusalem.
   a. mourned   b. flooded   c. destroyed

___ 15. God put _____ in Jeremiah's mouth.
   a. water   b. words   c. oil

___ 16. God said He would make Pashur a _____ to everyone around him.
   a. slave   b. threat   c. terror

___ 17. God was angry with His people because they _____.
   a. refused to work   b. served other gods   c. were unwilling to fight

___ 18. When Jehoiachin was king of Judah, the _____ army came and besieged Jerusalem.
   a. Canaanite   b. Babylonian   c. Egyptian

___ 19. They took away the king, his family, and _____ captives from the land of Judah.
   a. 10,000   b. 20,000   c. 30,000

___ 20. God said His people would be in captivity for _____ years.
   a. seven   b. seventy   c. seven hundred

(5 points each question)

SCORE _____

LESSON 34

DANIEL

CHOSEN CITY

JOHN WALSH

Search the Scriptures

Fill in the blanks

DANIEL 5:1-12

1. Belshazzar the _____ hosted a great feast for _____ of the lords in his kingdom.

2. While they were drinking wine, the king commanded to bring the _____ and _____ goblets that _____ had brought from the temple in Jerusalem.

3. Suddenly, there appeared _____ of a man's hand, writing on the _____ of the king's palace.

4. When Belshazzar saw it, he was so frightened that his knees _____.

5. He called for all the wise men of _____ and promised that whoever could read the writing and show him the interpretation would be clothed in _____, have a _____ _____ placed around his neck, and become the third highest ruler in the kingdom.

6. All the king's wise men came in, but none could _____.

7. Then the _____ suggested that the king call in _____.

DANIEL 5:13-31

8. When Daniel was brought in, he _____ the king's gifts but he promised to read the _____ and make known the _____ to the king.

9. He reminded Belshazzar that _____ had given Nebuchadnezzar great power and glory.

10. Nebuchadnezzar became filled with _____ and then he was driven from his _____.

11. He became like _____, he lived with wild donkeys, and he ate _____ like the cattle, until he recognized God's authority in his life.

12. Even though Belshazzar knew of Nebuchadnezzar's experience, he also refused to _____ himself before God.

THE WRITINGS AND THEIR INTERPRETATION:

13. Mene, Mene: God has _____ your kingdom and finished it.

14. Tekel: You are _____ in the _____ and found _____.

15. Upharsin (Peres): Your kingdom is _____ and given to the _____.

16. According to the king's command, Daniel was clothed in _____, given a _____ _____ around his neck, and made the _____ highest ruler in the kingdom.

17. That night, King Belshazzar was _____, and _____ took over the kingdom.

DANIEL 9:1-2

18. Daniel read the writings of _____ the prophet and learned that Jerusalem would be desolate for _____ years.

DANIEL 9:16-25

19. After confessing the sins of the nation, Daniel begged God to turn His anger away from the city of _____.

20. As Daniel was praying, he was visited by _____ who spoke with him and told him of the future of Jerusalem and about the coming of _____.

Scripture Crossword

DANIEL 5:1-31, DANIEL 9:1-2, DANIEL 9:16-25

ACROSS

2 King of Babylon
6 The king called for his ___ men to read the words.
8 Daniel read the prophecies of this man.
11 Belshazzar's banquet was for a ___ people.
14 Told Daniel about the future
17 The ___ of a man's hand appeared and began to write on the wall.
19 Belteshazzar
20 Mene
21 Upharsin (or) Peres

DOWN

1 Belshazzar decided to serve his guests wine in the sacred goblets from the ___ in Jerusalem.
3 man who became like a beast of the field
4 The king was so frightened that his ___ knocked together.
5 The ___ suggested the king send for Daniel.
6 Tekel
7 How old was Darius when he took over Babylon?
9 Daniel said to Belshazzar, "You have not ___ yourself."
10 The king put a ___ chain around Daniel's neck.
12 Another name for Xerxes
13 Conquering king of Babylon
15 Belshazzar was ___ the night of his feast.
16 The king offered to make Daniel the ___ highest in the kingdom.
18 Daniel told the king to ___ his gifts or give them to someone else.

Storyboard

Study the Storyboard until you can "see" the story

FIRST CLUSTER – Handwriting on the Wall

This part of the story is a simple narrative and is easy to remember. It is a story of the king going from an emotional high down to the depths of despair.

He takes three big steps down. It starts with Belshazzar having a feast and deciding to use the Temple vessels to honor his gods.

Step 1 – Fingers appear and write words on the wall.
Step 2 – Belshazzar becomes frantic and seeks help.
Step 3 – No help can be found.

Remember this by seeing the king happy lifting up a gold cup. His smile goes away when he sees fingers writing words. He looks around frantically, but can't find anyone to help.

King Belshazzar decided to have a feast with a thousand Babylonian nobles to celebrate their kingdom. He sent for the golden cups Nebuchadnezzar had taken from the Temple of God. They used these sacred cups to drink wine and toast their many gods.

Suddenly … the fingers of a man's hand appeared near a wall that was well lit by lamps. As Belshazzar watched, the fingers started writing on the wall. He became so terrified that his face turned white and his knees shook.

When the hand disappeared, Belshazzar called for all of his wise men and counselors. He said, "If you can interpret what these words mean, I will dress you in the finest clothes, drape you with gold jewelry, and make you the third ruler over Babylon!"

They looked at the writing but were unable to understand what it meant. This caused Belshazzar to tremble even more.

> ### Babylon
>
> *The outer walls of Babylon were 17 miles long, 22 feet thick, and 90 feet high, with guard towers another 100 feet high. The gates were made of bronze, and a system of inner and outer walls and moats made the city very secure. Therefore Belshazzar thought he was safe, even when the Medo-Persian army surrounded Babylon.*

SECOND CLUSTER – Calling for Daniel

Picture three people – the king, the Queen Mother, and Daniel. The queen provides comfort to her son, and points to the prophet. The king turns to Daniel and offers gifts for his help. The prophet refuses the gifts. Before interpreting the words on the wall, He reminds Belshazzar that:

Nebuchadnezzar honored God. (The story is in Daniel 4.)

Belshazzar had offended God.

The Queen Mother came and said, "Don't be fearful. There is one counselor you have not called. His name is Daniel, and he is a man filled with the Spirit of God. Nebuchadnezzar had great respect for him and called on him whenever he had a problem he could not solve. He will tell you what this mystery means."

Belshazzar called for Daniel and said to him, "I know you have the Spirit of God dwelling in you. If you can tell me what this means, I will dress you in the finest clothes, drape you with gold jewelry, and make you the third ruler over Babylon."

Daniel did not hesitate to answer the king. "You may keep your fine gifts and give your titles to others. I will read the writing and tell you what it means."

"God gave Nebuchadnezzar this empire and made him the most powerful man on earth. Yet he learned to humble himself before God and acknowledged that He was Lord of all."

"You know all of this, yet you are proud and defy the Lord God. You sent for the golden cups from the Temple of God, and used them to praise false gods. You mocked the God who holds your life in His hands. Therefore He has sent you this message."

THIRD CLUSTER – A Message from God

The words on the wall were not a foreign language for the king. He understood the words, but he didn't know what message they represented.

The key to remember this part of the story is to see the picture God is giving the king. God is holding the kingdom in His hand while looking at a calendar. He then looks at a scale with His tolerance on one side, and the king's worth is on the other. The king's worth is too light. He was found lacking. God disapproves, shakes his head in disgust, and hands the kingdom to someone else. The message Daniel gave the king was devastating, yet Daniel is given great wealth. The kingdom changes hands by morning.

"NUMBERED, NUMBERED, WEIGHED, AND DIVIDED."

Daniel spoke, "Here is the interpretation:

NUMBERED – *God has numbered the days of your kingdom and time has run out.*

WEIGHED – *You were weighed on a scale to determine your worth, and you have been found lacking.*

DIVIDED – *Your kingdom is no longer yours. It has been divided between the Medes and Persians."*

Immediately, Belshazzar called his servants and ordered them to put the finest clothes on Daniel. They put expensive jewelry around his neck, and Belshazzar proclaimed him the third ruler over Babylon.

That very night, the army of the Medes and Persians came into the city, killed Belshazzar, and took over the kingdom.

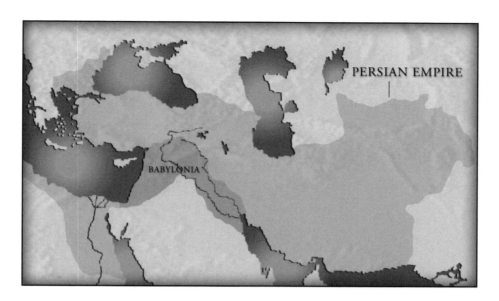

The Persian Empire around 500 B.C.

When the city of Babylon was conquered, Babylonia became a comparatively small part of the Persian empire, which then stretched all the way from India to Ethopia and Europe. The Persian empire encompassed all of the civilized world except for Greece.

FOURTH CLUSTER – Years Later

The most difficult part of this cluster to remember is the breakdown of the 490 years. This chart will help.

Daniel became a respected counselor in the Persian court. Years later, he was reading the writings of Jeremiah that said Jerusalem would lie in ruins for seventy years. God sent him an angel to explain what would happen after that time.

He said, "The order to rebuild Jerusalem will begin a special 490-year period of time for your people. Messiah will come after 483 years. He will be killed and Jerusalem will be destroyed again. The last seven years will begin when an evil ruler makes a seven-year peace agreement with many nations and Israel."

With this, God showed to Daniel what was going to happen with Israel until the time that He sets up His kingdom upon earth.

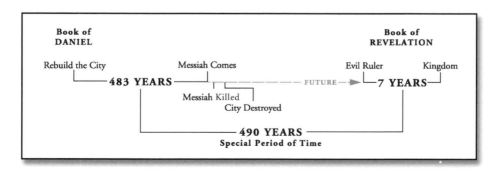

Telling the Story

DANIEL

HANDWRITING ON THE WALL

King Belshazzar decided to have a feast with a thousand Babylonian nobles to celebrate their kingdom. He sent for the golden cups Nebuchadnezzar had taken from the Temple of God. They used these sacred cups to drink wine and toast their many gods.

Suddenly … the fingers of a man's hand appeared near a wall that was well lit by lamps. As Belshazzar watched, the fingers started writing on the wall. He became so terrified that his face turned white and his knees shook.

When the hand disappeared, Belshazzar called for all of his wise men and counselors. He said, "If you can interpret what these words mean, I will dress you in the finest clothes, drape you with gold jewelry, and make you the third ruler over Babylon!"

They looked at the writing but were unable to understand what it meant. This caused Belshazzar to tremble even more.

CALLING FOR DANIEL

The Queen Mother came and said, "Don't be fearful. There is one counselor you have not called. His name is Daniel, and he is a man filled with the Spirit of God. Nebuchadnezzar had great respect for him and called on him whenever he had a problem he could not solve. He will tell you what this mystery means."

Belshazzar called for Daniel and said to him, "I know

you have the Spirit of God dwelling in you. If you can tell me what this means, I will dress you in the finest clothes, drape you with gold jewelry, and make you the third ruler over Babylon."

Daniel did not hesitate to answer the king. "You may keep your fine gifts and give your titles to others. I will read the writing and tell you what it means."

"God gave Nebuchadnezzar this empire and made him the most powerful man on earth. Yet he learned to humble himself before God and acknowledged that He was Lord of all."

"You know all of this, yet you are proud and defy the Lord God. You sent for the golden cups from the Temple of God, and used them to praise false gods. You mocked the God who holds your life in His hands. Therefore He has sent you this message."

A MESSAGE FROM GOD

"NUMBERED, NUMBERED, WEIGHED, AND DIVIDED."

Daniel spoke, "Here is the interpretation:

NUMBERED – God has numbered the days of your kingdom and time has run out.

WEIGHED – You were weighed on a scale to determine your worth, and you have been found lacking.

DIVIDED – Your kingdom is no longer yours. It has been divided between the Medes and Persians."

Immediately, Belshazzar called his servants and ordered them to put the finest clothes on Daniel. They put expensive jewelry around his neck, and Belshazzar proclaimed him the third ruler over Babylon.

That very night, the army of the Medes and Persians came into the city, killed Belshazzar, and took over the kingdom.

YEARS LATER

Daniel became a respected counselor in the Persian court. Years later, he was reading the writings of Jeremiah that said Jerusalem would lie in ruins for seventy years. God sent him an angel to explain what would happen after that time.

He said, "The order to rebuild Jerusalem will begin a special 490-year period of time for your people. Messiah will come after 483 years. He will be killed and Jerusalem will be destroyed again. The last seven years will begin when an evil ruler makes a seven-year peace agreement with many nations and Israel."

With this, God showed to Daniel what was going to happen with Israel until the time that He sets up His kingdom upon earth.

Extra Storyboard

First
Cluster

Second
Cluster

Third
Cluster

Fourth
Cluster

Activities

Using the boxes below, give the storyboard in words or pictures.

First Cluster	Second Cluster
Third Cluster	Fourth Cluster

Feel free to use blank pages to write down or draw additional clusters or ideas.

What did you learn about **God** from the story of *Daniel?*

_____

_____

_____

What did you learn about **people** from the story of *Daniel?*

_____

_____

_____

What was your **favorite** part of the story? Tell why.

_____

_____

_____

PROVERB: a pithy statement that helps you remember an important truth. Create a proverb based on this story.

_____

_____

BANNER OR BUMPER STICKER: Give the essence of this story in six words or less.

ACTIVITIES: Choose from the following, or create another activity that helps you learn the story.

Drama
- Act out Belshazzar's feast. For writing on the wall, use a chalkboard with chalk already on it. Use a finger to "write" words.

Dramatic Monologue
- Tell the first-person story of Belshazzar's Grandfather (Nebuchadnezzar) found in Daniel 4.

Storytelling
- Use puppets to tell this story.
- Tell the story from the point of view of one of the servants who served at the feast and who later served the king of Persia.

Poetry
- Write a poem about Belshazzar's feast and the turn of events afterwards.
- Perform a dramatic reading or recitation of the poem *Vision of Belshazzar* by Lord Byron.
- Perform a dramatic reading or recitation of the poem *Belshazzar* by Heinrich Hein

Research
- Give a report on the emphasis put upon dreams in the culture of Daniel's time.
- Do a study of the 490 years Daniel prophesied about. Show what things have already happened and explain what remains to be fulfilled in the future.

Writing
- Rewrite the story as if it were the diary of the Queen Mother.
- Write an essay on the highlights of Daniel's life and the various kings with whom he interacted.
- Tell what it means today when people say, "The handwriting is on the wall."
- List at least ten other slogans (based on Biblical ideas) that are commonly used in today's world.

Discussion
- Discuss the attitudes and character qualities Daniel demonstrated and how they elevated his position while he was in captivity.

TIE TO PREVIOUS STORY: Write how you would connect this story with the previous story.

_____

_____

_____

TELL THE STORY: To whom did you tell the story and what was their response?

_____

_____

Quiz 34

Name _____

TRUE OR FALSE

Date _____

___ 1. Belshazzar the king hosted a great _____ for the officials in his kingdom.
    a. sacrifice   b. feast   c. dance

___ 2. The king commanded to bring out the _____ that Nebuchadnezzar had brought from Jerusalem.
    a. temple goblets   b. Hebrew captives   c. golden images

___ 3. Suddenly, there appeared a ____ writing on the wall.
    a. flaming sword   b. shining angel   c. man's hand

___ 4. When Belshazzar saw it, he was so frightened that _____.
    a. his knees knocked   b. he fainted   c. he wept loudly

___ 5. He called for all the _____ of his kingdom.
    a. prophets   b. women   c. wise men

___ 6. He offered _____ for whoever could read the writing and show him the interpretation of it.
    a. riches and honor   b. pardon   c. large plot of land

___ 7. All the king's _____ came in, but none could help.
    a. children   b. wise men   c. scribes

___ 8. Then the _____ told the king about Daniel.
    a. queen   b. governor   c. prince

___ 9. Daniel was described as having within him the spirit of _____.
    a. humility   b. knowledge   c. God

___ 10. The king promised him _____ if he could do what the other wise men could not do.
    a. gifts and power   b. wives and concubines   c. houses and lands

___ 11. Daniel _____ what the king offered.
    a. accepted   b. negotiated   c. refused

___ 12. He reminded Belshazzar that the _____ had given Nebuchadnezzar great power and glory.
    a. king of Persia   b. most high God   c. nobles of Babylon

___ 13. Nebuchadnezzar became filled with _____, and then he was deposed and driven from his throne.
    a. pride   b. illness   c. pain

___ 14. He lived like a wild beast and ate _____ like the cattle, until he recognized God's authority in his life.
    a. corn   b. beans   c. grass

___ 15. Like his ancestor Nebuchadnezzar, Belshazzar also had great _____.
    a. humility   b. pride   c. knowledge

___ 16. God revealed to Belshazzar that his kingdom would _____.
    a. endure for ever   b. be given to another   c. be honored by God

___ 17. According to the king's command, Daniel was _____.
    a. promoted   b. punished   c. killed

___ 18. That night, King Belshazzar was _____.
    a. carried away captive   b. killed   c. healed

___ 19. Daniel read the writings of _____ to learn about the future of Jerusalem.
    a. the king's wise men   b. Persian history   c. Jeremiah

___ 20. As Daniel was praying, he was visited by Gabriel and told about the coming _____.
    a. kingdom   b. famine   c. Messiah

(5 points each question)

SCORE _____

LESSON 35

REBUILDING THE TEMPLE

CHOSEN CITY

JOHN WALSH

Search the Scriptures

Fill in the blanks

EZRA 1:1-11

1. Cyrus the king of _____ made a proclamation that God's people should go to _____, which is in _____, and rebuild the House of the Lord.

2. Those who were not going to help were to give _____, _____, goods, animals, and free-will _____ to help in the project.

3. Also, _____ the king brought out all the articles of the House of the Lord that _____ had taken from Jerusalem. When his treasurer counted them, he found a total of _____ altogether!

EZRA 2:1-2, 64-70

4. The total number in this group of people who came up out of captivity and returned to Jerusalem and Judah was _____.

5. There were also over 7,000 _____, including 200 _____.

6. They had thousands of animals including _____, _____, _____, and donkeys.

EZRA 3:1-6

7. When the Israelites were gathered together at _____, they set up an _____ to God and offered burnt offerings on it both _____ and _____.

8. However, the _____ of the temple was not yet laid.

EZRA 3:7-13

9. The Israelites paid the _____ and _____ and they gave food and drink to the people of Sidon and Tyre in exchange for receiving _____ trees from _____.

10. In the second month of the second _____ after they returned, Zerubbabel and Jeshua, and the people began working on the _____ of the _____.

11. When the builders got the _____ of the temple laid, the priests and Levites played on their _____ and _____.

12. The people _____ together, giving praise and thanks to the _____ because He is _____ and His mercy endures forever.

13. All the people _____ loudly as they praised the Lord for the foundation of the Temple being laid.

14. Many of the _____ men who had seen Solomon's Temple _____ with a loud voice as they looked at the foundation of this building, and many _____ aloud with _____.

EZRA 4:1-5

15. When the _____ of the returned captives heard that the Temple was being rebuilt, they came and asked to help with the project.

16. Zerubbabel (the governor of Judah) _____ their help, so they began to make _____.

EZRA 5:1-2

17. The prophets _____ and Zechariah prophesied to the Jews in Judah and
_____.

18. Once again, _____ and his men began to _____ the House of God.

EZRA 6:1-22

19. _____ the king made a decree that the work should go forward.

20. The king also provided them young _____ and _____ and _____ for the
sacrifices (burnt offerings) to the God of Heaven.

21. When the house of God was finished, they had a dedication service, offered _____,
ate the Passover, and celebrated the Feast of _____.

HAGGAI 1:1-8

22. The word of the _____ came through Haggai: "God's people are living in beautiful finished
_____, while the house of the _____ is still not built."

23. "As a result, they sow much and bring in _____; they _____ but are still hungry; they
_____ but are not satisfied; they put on clothes but are not _____; the money they
earn goes into a bag with _____."

24. Haggai's challenge: "_____ your ways!"

25. Haggai told the people to go up to the _____, get wood and build the Lord's _____.

HAGGAI 2:1-9

26. God said that even if this temple is not as glorious as the _____ one, the day will come when
"the Desire of all nations" shall come and God will fill this house with _____.

27. The glory of the _____ house will be greater than the glory of the _____.

Cedars of Lebanon

- Among all the trees in Lebanon, the most famous and most treasured species is the Cedar of Lebanon.
- Often reaching a height of over 100 feet, it is quite wide with branches growing nearly straight out.
- For thousands of years its timber has been highly prized for building king's houses and palaces.
- Its superb qualities include its hardness, beautiful color and exquisite fragrance, as well as its resistance to insects, humidity and temperature.
- The masts of ships in the seaport city of Tyre were made with Cedar beams.
- Because the wood seemed to be nearly indestructible, the Cedar of Lebanon came to symbolize strength and magnificence.
- Today, the majestic Cedar tree is the emblem of Lebanon and adorns its flag, which was adopted in 1943.

Scripture Crossword

EZRA 1:1-11, EZRA 2:1-2, 64-70, EZRA 3:1-13, EZRA 4:1-5, EZRA 5:1-2, EZRA 6:1-22
HAGGAI 1:1-8, HAGGAI 2:1-9

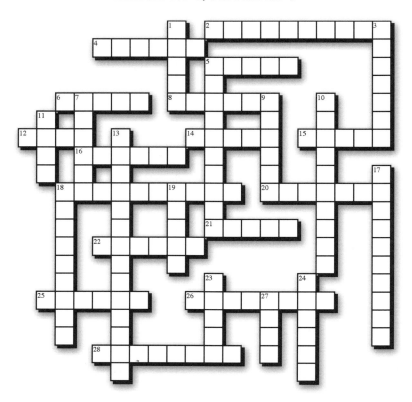

ACROSS

2 After the temple was completed, the people celebrated the Feast of ____ Bread.
4 King who ordered the enemies to help pay for the temple work.
5 King of Persia
6 The Lord said, "I will fill this House with ____."
8 The people returning to Judah took with them 736 ____.
12 Some older people ____ when they saw the foundation for the new temple.
14 Came from Lebanon
15 The people returning to Judah took with them 245 ____.
16 Levites had to be at least this age before working in the House of the Lord.
18 Who was in charge of the rebuilding?
20 The glory of the current temple would be ____ than that of the old one.
21 The temple was completed in the __ year of Darius' reign.
22 prophet who spoke of "bags with holes"
25 Darius ordered that anyone hindering the work on the temple would be ____.

26 Who prophesied the captivity would last 70 years?
28 Shortly after the temple was completed, the Israelites celebrated the ____.

DOWN

1 Governor of ___: Zerubbabel.
3 The people returning to Judah took with them 6,720 ____.
5 The Israelites hired masons and ____.
7 The Lord's message to the people: "You expect much, but you receive ____."
9 The Lord said, "Be ____ and work."
10 There was great rejoicing when the ____ of the temple was laid.
11 The enemies of the Israelites offered to ____ with the building.
13 The decree of Cyrus said that treasures taken by ____ were to be returned.
17 Kings of Persia: Cyrus, Darius and ____.
18 Two prophets: Haggai and ____.
19 ____ was built on the temple site
23 God said, "In this place I will grant ____."
24 The people returning to Judah took with them 435 ____.
27 God said, "The silver and gold is ____."

Storyboard

Study the Storyboard until you can "see" the story

FIRST CLUSTER – Time to Build

Pantomime the following to remember the happenings of this cluster. The king of Persia is giving a proclamation while standing behind a table. On the table are coins (gold & silver), sacred vessels, and cedar boards. The king then picks up a lamb (sacrifice). Some people go, while others give money.

The people arrive, build an altar, sacrifice a lamb, and shout. This irritates those who are already there, so they go to the new king. He shakes his finger (no-no). The people stop building, pick up cedar to put in their own houses, and say, "This is not a good time to build."

Jeremiah's prophecy had said the captivity of God's people would end after 70 years. When the time was fulfilled, God moved the king of Persia to make a proclamation. "The Lord has commanded me to send His people back to Jerusalem so they can rebuild the Temple. Therefore, they are free to go to Judah and build the House of God."

He sent gold and silver to pay for the project, and gave back the Temple vessels taken when Jerusalem was destroyed. He provided money to buy cedar from Lebanon to panel the inside of the Temple. He even provided livestock so the people could make sacrifices to God.

The Lord stirred the hearts of His people and many moved back to Judah to do the work of God. Those who could not go gave money and supplies.

When the people arrived, they built an altar on the Temple site. The priests made sacrifices to God and the people shouted for joy and gave praise. They then organized themselves to begin building the Temple.

Those living around Jerusalem were concerned when they saw the Jewish people back in the land. They did everything they could to stop them from building the Temple. Finally when there was a new king in Persia, they sent a message to him and slanted the news about what was happening in Jerusalem. They convinced him to stop the construction.

The builders were discouraged when they were forced to stop. Still, there was nothing they could do but wait for a change in the situation. They concentrated on establishing their own houses.

Soon it became evident that one family after another began having cedar paneling inside of their homes. Eventually the stockpile of cedar from Lebanon was gone! It could not be replaced, so no one wanted to think about building the Temple. They simply said, "This is not a good time to build."

SECOND CLUSTER – Get Back to Work

Haggai gives two sermons on "sowing and reaping," the first is negative and the second is positive. The first **sowing & reaping** sermon gives five illustrations to show how the people were not getting what they wanted:

       1) planting – no harvest
       2) eating – hunger
       3) drinking – thirst
       4) clothes – cold
       5) money – bags with holes

You can remember these five illustrations by envisioning you are holding a seed (planting) that becomes a piece of bread (eating). In the other hand you have a drink of water (drinking).

These disappear as you put your hands on your clothes (clothes). Reach into two pockets and pull out a coin and small bag. Put the coin in the bag, which falls out the bottom (bags with holes).

The people look at the spot where the cedar had been. Haggai points to the hills and the people go get plain wood and start building.

A prophet named Haggai came to the people and said, "I have a message from the Lord! 'Consider your ways! You say it is not time to build the House of God. Yet you live in paneled houses while My house lies in ruins. Consider your ways!'"

He told them God had removed His blessing from their lives. "You plant a large amount of grain, yet you harvest very little. You eat, but you're still hungry. You drink, but you're still thirsty. You wear clothes, yet you're not warm. You earn wages, and put your money into bags — bags that have holes. Consider your ways!"

As the people listened, they realized they had no cedar with which to finish the Temple. Haggai said, "God wants you to build His house. Therefore, go into the hills and get common wood and use that in the Temple. God says He will be pleased with what you build, and He will be glorified."

So the people obeyed the prophet and went into the hills and got wood to replace the missing cedar. Once that issue was settled, they made preparations to restart the project.

God put another king on the Persian throne. This one gave the order, "Anyone who opposes the building of the Temple will be put to death!" Now those who lived around Jerusalem were not allowed to hinder the construction of the Temple. Instead, they were commanded to give supplies for its completion.

THIRD CLUSTER – Finishing the Job

The second **sowing & reaping** sermon was an encouraging message. Haggai told them how they did not plant, but harvested anyway. He used three types of harvest – seed, vines, and trees. You can remember this because it goes from smaller to larger.

The prophet gives an encouraging message, but some of the old men give a discouraging message. They began reminiscing about the old days and how awful the new temple was. Haggai told them about the glory and future of that temple.

This is a great prophecy, so use your hands to remember the details. Envision the temple on one side and the nations on the other. Point at the temple. It becomes bigger and more beautiful. (Its glory will be greater.)

Turn, grab the nations, and shake them (shake the nations). Now sweep your hands back towards the Temple so the world can focus on it (world will focus on this spot). Move your hands up to show glory (I will fill this Temple with glory). Now bring your hands back down as if you are getting back to work (focus on your work). These hand gestures are complex, so practice them until you can give this prophecy.

The people worked with enthusiasm and Haggai came with another message from the Lord. "I am pleased you have obeyed My word! Look, ... I am blessing you and providing for you. You have not planted your seed, your vines have not yet brought forth grapes, and your trees have not bloomed. Yet you are harvesting My blessings and provisions. And I will continue to bless you."

As the building was nearing completion, most of the people rejoiced, but some of the older men moaned and cried. "We remember Solomon's Temple. It was so beautiful! This Temple is so small ... and ... it's not beautiful at all." The builders became discouraged.

God sent Haggai with another message. "Who remembers the Temple built by Solomon? How does this one compare to it? Be encouraged! The glory of this Temple is going to be greater than you can imagine. I am going to shake the nations and the whole world will focus on this very spot. The 'Desire of all Nations' will come and I will fill this Temple with glory. Be strong and keep your eyes focused on the present work. I am with you as I have always been."

So the people were encouraged ... and worked ... and they finished the Temple.

Telling the Story
REBUILDING THE TEMPLE

TIME TO BUILD

Jeremiah's prophecy had said the captivity of God's people would end after 70 years. When the time was fulfilled, God moved the king of Persia to make a proclamation. "The Lord has commanded me to send His people back to Jerusalem so they can rebuild the Temple. Therefore, they are free to go to Judah and build the House of God."

The king sent gold and silver to pay for the project, and gave back the Temple vessels taken when Jerusalem was destroyed. He provided money to buy cedar from Lebanon to panel the inside of the Temple. He even provided livestock so the people could make sacrifices to God. The Lord stirred the hearts of His people and many moved back to Judah to do the work of God. Those who could not go gave money and supplies.

When the people arrived, they built an altar on the Temple site. The priests made sacrifices to God and the people shouted for joy and gave praise. They then organized themselves to begin building the Temple.

Those living around Jerusalem were concerned when they saw the Jewish people back in the land. They did everything they could to stop them from building the Temple. Finally when there was a new king in Persia, they sent a message to him and slanted the news about what was happening in Jerusalem. They convinced him to stop the construction.

The builders were discouraged when they were forced to stop. Still, there was nothing they could do but wait for a change in the situation. They concentrated on establishing their own houses. Before long, it became evident that one family after another began having cedar paneling inside of their homes. Eventually the stockpile of cedar from Lebanon was gone! It could not be replaced, so no one wanted to think about building the Temple. They simply said, "This is not a good time to build."

GET BACK TO WORK

A prophet named Haggai came to the people and said, "I have a message from the Lord! 'Consider your ways! You say it is not time to build the House of God. Yet you live in paneled houses while My house lies in ruins. Consider your ways!' "

Haggai told them that God had removed His blessing from their lives. "You plant a large amount of grain, yet you harvest very little. You eat, but you're still hungry. You drink, but you're still thirsty. You wear clothes, yet you're not warm. You earn wages, and put your money into bags – bags that have holes. Consider your ways!"

As the people listened, they realized they had no cedar with which to finish the Temple. Haggai said, "God wants you to build His house. Therefore, go into the hills and get common wood and use that in the Temple. God says He will be pleased with what you build, and He will be glorified." So the people obeyed the prophet and went into the hills and got wood to replace the missing cedar. Once that issue was settled, they made preparations to restart the project.

God put another king on the Persian throne. This one gave the order, "Anyone who opposes the building of the Temple will be put to death!" Now those who lived around Jerusalem were not allowed to hinder the construction of the Temple. Instead, they were commanded to give supplies for its completion.

FINISHING THE JOB

The people worked with enthusiasm and Haggai came with another message from the Lord. "I am pleased you have obeyed My word! Look, … I am blessing you and providing for you. You have not planted your seed, your vines have not yet brought forth grapes, and your trees have not bloomed. Yet you are harvesting My blessings and provisions. And I will continue to bless you."

As the building was nearing completion, most of the people rejoiced, but some of the older men moaned and cried. "We remember Solomon's Temple. It was so beautiful! This Temple is so small … and … it's not beautiful at all." The builders became discouraged.

God sent Haggai with another message. "Who remembers the Temple built by Solomon? How does this one compare to it? Be encouraged! The glory of this Temple is going to be greater than you can imagine. I am going to shake the nations and the whole world will focus on this very spot. The 'Desire of all Nations' will come and I will fill this Temple with glory. Be strong and keep your eyes focused on the present work. I am with you as I have always been."

So the people were encouraged … and worked … and they finished the Temple.

Extra Storyboard

First
Cluster

Second
Cluster

Third
Cluster

Activities

Using the boxes below, give the storyboard in words or pictures.

First Cluster	Second Cluster	Third Cluster

Feel free to use blank pages to write down or draw additional clusters or ideas.

What did you learn about **God** from the story of *Rebuilding the Temple?*

_____

_____

_____

What did you learn about **people** from the story of *Rebuilding the Temple?*

_____

_____

_____

What was your **favorite** part of the story? Tell why.

_____

_____

_____

PROVERB: a pithy statement that helps you remember an important truth. Create a proverb based on this story.

_____

_____

BANNER OR BUMPER STICKER: Give the essence of this story in six words or less.

ACTIVITIES: Choose from the following, or create another activity that helps you learn the story.

Drama
- Act out Haggai's three visits to those rebuilding the temple. Include how the emotions of the people changed with each message.
- A news reporter talks about events leading up to the re-building project. Interview the leader (Zerubbabel) and some of the workers. Ask about what has happened so far and their expectation for the days to come.

Storytelling
- Tell the events of this story in the first-person as the prophet Haggai.

Group Activity
- "Who Said It?" Give quotes by the various characters in the story. Don't worry about exact wording, but express the "gist" of what was probably said. (King Cyrus, Zerubabel, the builders, enemies, Haggai, people taking wood from stockpile, King Artaxerxes, King Darius)

Poetry
- Put the prophet Haggai's message into a poem.

Music
- Create music to go with the lyrics written in the Poetry section.
- Perform a song of praise about God's enduring mercy. Include as many of the events from this story as possible. Psalm 136 shows an example of how this might be done. Include accompaniment with trumpets, cymbals, or other suitable instruments.

Art
- Make side-by-side drawings of how you envision Solomon's temple and the re-built temple of Haggai's time.

Research/Writing
- Study interesting facts in the life of Zerubabel and give a report.
- Report on the three kings who ordered the rebuilding of the Temple – Cyrus, Artaxerxes, and Darius.

Discussion
- Discuss the statement that "The heart of the king is in the hand of the Lord." Tell how this truth is evident in previous stories and in this one. Give examples of how God hardened the hearts of some kings and softened the hearts of others.

TIE TO PREVIOUS STORY: Write how you would connect this story with the previous story.

_____

_____

_____

TELL THE STORY: To whom did you tell the story and what was their response?

_____

_____

_____

Quiz 35

Name _____

Date _____

TRUE OR FALSE

____ 1. The prophecy from Jeremiah said the captivity of God's people would end after seven years.

____ 2. When the time was fulfilled, God moved the king of Persia to proclaim that the Jews could go back to Jerusalem and rebuild the House of the Lord.

____ 3. He gave back the articles taken from the Temple when the Babylonians destroyed the city.

____ 4. He provided payment for getting cedar from Lebanon to panel the inside of the Temple.

____ 5. He even provided fruits and vegetables so the people could make sacrifices to God.

____ 6. Many of the Lord's people moved back to Judah to do the work of God.

____ 7. When the people arrived, they built an altar and the priests made sacrifices to God.

____ 8. The other nationalities of people living around Jerusalem were pleased to have the Jewish people back in the land.

____ 9. They did everything they could to help with the building project.

____ 10. After the foundation was laid, a new king in Persia ordered the people to stop building the Temple.

____ 11. So the people concentrated on establishing their own personal houses.

____ 12. Even after all the families put cedar paneling inside their homes, there was still plenty of lumber in the stockpile of cedar from Lebanon.

____ 13. No one wanted to think about building the Temple. They simply said, "This is not a good time to build."

____ 14. The prophet Nathan came to the people and said, "I have a message from the Lord! You say it is not time to build the House of God. Yet you live in paneled houses while My house lies in ruins. Consider your ways!'"

____ 15. The prophet Haggai told them that God had removed His blessing from their lives.

____ 16. Since the people had no more cedar with which to finish the Temple, Haggai told them to go into the hills and get common wood and use that to build the Temple.

____ 17. So the people made preparations to restart the project.

____ 18. Meanwhile, God raised up another king of Persia who favored the building of the Temple.

____ 19. As the building was nearing completion, the young people started to moan and cry. "We remember Solomon's Temple. It was so beautiful – much more beautiful than this temple!"

____ 20. Then Haggai came with another message from God. "Be encouraged! Someday, the glory of this Temple is going to be greater than that of the first Temple."

(5 points each question)   SCORE _____

LESSON 36

NEHEMIAH

CHOSEN CITY

JOHN WALSH

Search the Scriptures

Fill in the blanks

NEHEMIAH 1:1-11

1. Nehemiah wept and mourned when he received a report that the wall of Jerusalem was _____ and its gates were _____.

2. Nehemiah remembered that God had said to Moses that if His people turned against Him, He would _____; but if His people would turn their hearts toward Him and obey His commandments, God would _____.

3. Nehemiah was the king's _____, and he asked God to grant him favor with the king.

NEHEMIAH 2:1-18

4. When King _____ saw how sad Nehemiah was, he asked what he wanted to request.

5. Nehemiah requested that the king send him to _____.

6. He asked for _____ to the governors so that he could pass through safely to _____.

7. He also asked for a letter to Asaph, the _____, asking for _____ to make beams for the _____, for the _____ of the city, and for his _____.

8. The king sent with Nehemiah captains of the _____ and _____.

9. Sanballat and Tobiah were _____ about Nehemiah's presence in Jerusalem.

10. Nehemiah went out during the _____ to inspect the walls of Jerusalem.

11. Nehemiah encouraged the Jewish priests, nobles, and rulers to rise up and build the _____ around Jerusalem, so that it would no longer be a _____.

NEHEMIAH 4:1-8, 14-18

12. When Sanballat heard that the Jews were building the wall, he was _____.

13. Tobiah also mocked saying, "If a _____ goes up on their stone wall, he will break it down."

14. Sanballat and Tobiah conspired to _____ against those who were re-building the wall.

15. Nehemiah encouraged the people saying, "Do not be _____ of them; remember the Lord… and fight for your brothers, your _____, your _____, your _____, and your _____."

16. From that time forth, as the Jews worked on the wall, they also kept their _____ with them.

NEHEMIAH 6:1-4, 15-16

17. Sanballat, Tobiah, and their people repeatedly asked Nehemiah to _____.

18. Nehemiah replied, _____.

19. The wall was completed in _____ days, and even the _____ of the Jews recognized that the work on the _____ was completed with the help of _____.

NEHEMIAH 7:4, 8:1-3, 11:1-2

20. Jerusalem was _____, but there were few _____ living there because the houses were not rebuilt.

21. All the people gathered in front of the water gate, and _____ read to them from the Book of the _____ of Moses, from _____ until noon.

22. One out of _____ people were chosen to live in Jerusalem.

Scripture Crossword

NEH.1:1-11, NEH.2:1-18, NEH.4:1-18, NEH.6:1-16, NEH.7:4, NEH.8:1-3, NEH.11:1-2

ACROSS

3 Nehemiah's enemies asked ___ times if he would come for a meeting.

5 Nehemiah's brother

7 The enemies realized the work had been done with the help of ___.

8 Tobiah said that even a ___ could break down the wall.

10 Nehemiah reminded God of His words spoken to ___.

12 Nehemiah's enemies asked him to come and ___ with them.

13 Nehemiah told the people, "Don't be ___."

14 When Nehemiah heard his brother's report, he sat down and ___.

17 Ezra read aloud from daybreak until ___.

19 Nehemiah wanted to ___ the wall.

21 Scribe/Priest

22 The people were ___ as Ezra read.

24 The city was ___.

25 The Israelites kept their _ with them while they worked.

28 It ___ the king to send Nehemiah to Judah.

30 The king ___ Nehemiah's requests.

31 One in ___ Israelites chose to live in Jerusalem.

DOWN

1 Nehemiah's job

2 The king asked Nehemiah why he looked ___.

3 The wall was completed in ___ days.

4 Before Nehemiah answered the king's question, he ___.

5 Even though the wall around Jerusalem was rebuilt, the people's ___ were not yet built.

6 The king sent officers of the ___ and the cavalry with Nehemiah.

9 During the conversation with Nehemiah, who was sitting next to the king?

11 The people assembled at the ___ gate to hear the reading.

15 When the wall was completed, the ___ were depressed.

16 The report was that the wall of Jerusalem was ___ down.

18 The gates of Jerusalem had been ___.

20 Nehemiah asked the king to give him ___ to the governors.

23 Nehemiah mourned, ___ and prayed.

26 Nehemiah inspected the walls of Jerusalem at ___.

27 Nehemiah was afraid to tell the ___ why he was sad.

29 Ezra read from the Book of the ___ of Moses.

Storyboard

Study the Storyboard until you can "see" the story

FIRST CLUSTER – Getting Permission to Build

This cluster has two "thinks & talks" The first "think & talk" is when Nehemiah gets the news about Jerusalem. Thinking about it makes him depressed. He then talks to God and the king. The king gives him three things: permission, travel papers, and timber for construction.

The second "think & talk" was when he went to Jerusalem. He spends three days looking over the city and not telling anyone what he is thinking about. He then talks to the leaders and tells them about his plan. He tells them three things. "God's for it, the king's for it, now let's build it."

It is important to remember how the leaders responded. They agreed it was time to rebuild the wall, divided the wall into smaller sections, and organized their people to build one section.

Nehemiah served the king of Persia. He received news that his people in Judah were suffering and the walls of Jerusalem were in ruins. Sorrow overcame Nehemiah, and he sat down and cried. He was depressed for several days and prayed that God would help his people.

The king asked him why he was so sad. Nehemiah stood before him and told him about the situation in Jerusalem. The king was moved and said, "How can I help?"

"Oh please, send me to Jerusalem and give me permission to rebuild the walls."

The king said he could go, and issued letters for safe travel. He was given access to the royal forest near Jerusalem for building materials.

Nehemiah traveled to the city and spent the first three days looking over the situation. He did not tell the people what he had in mind, but went out at night to see the city ruins. Finally he brought the leaders together and told them how God had burdened his heart. He explained how the king of Persia had given permission for rebuilding the city walls.

Nehemiah said, "We cannot live with this disgrace any longer. It is time to rebuild the walls!" All of the leaders of the land looked at one another and then enthusiastically agreed. They committed themselves to this project, and each one chose a section of the wall that would be his responsibility. They then went out and organized their people to build it.

SECOND CLUSTER – Trying to Stop the Builders

This cluster can be divided into the two sections, the attacks and Nehemiah's encouragement. The two attacks include – Mocking & Threats.

Mocking: The key here is the joke they tell about the fox. The people are discouraged but they keep working, and half the wall goes up.

Threats: The workers hear that their lives are in danger. They develop a plan to protect themselves. Review that plan.

Nehemiah's Encouragement: "Don't be discouraged, and be prepared to fight." He tells them what they should be willing to fight for – their countrymen, sons, daughters, wives, and homes. (Remember, two males, two females, and home.)

The non-Jewish people of the area were angry when they saw what was happening. They decided they must try to stop the construction. They told jokes about the builders and laughed at them. They said, "These people are too weak to rebuild their city. Ha! I can see it now. They build a section of wall, and the whole thing falls down when a little fox jumps on it."

This was discouraging for the builders, but they were determined and worked faster. Soon the wall was half way up. They started joining the various sections together, which made their enemies furious. Those who opposed the building of the wall knew they had to act quickly if they were to stop the construction. They threatened to sneak up and kill the workers. They said, "We will do whatever it takes to stop this wall!"

Fear gripped the hearts of the builders, so they set up guards to watch day and night. Nehemiah encouraged them. "Don't be afraid. God is stronger than your enemies. Be prepared to fight! Fight for your fellow Jews. Fight for your sons and daughters. Fight for your wives and homes."

The workers prepared to fight from that day on. They set up a warning system in case there was an attack on any section of the wall. Men were prepared to respond quickly and rush to that area and fight.

THIRD CLUSTER – Finishing the Wall

The first part of this cluster is easy to remember: The walls are up, except for gates. The enemies decide to kill Nehemiah, so they send letters inviting him to meet with them in a nearby village. Envision Nehemiah working when he gets the invitation. "I am doing a great work." He shrugs, "Why should I leave this to talk to you?" The response he gets is, "Because if you don't, we are gong to tell!"

The end of this story is important to remember because it shows the commitment of the people. The following hand gestures will help.

> Hold up five fingers, and then reduce them down to two
> > – fifty-two days from start to finish.
> Put both hands up like you are rejoicing
> > – They rejoiced and sang praise to God.
> Bring both hands together like you are reading a book
> > – They read the Scriptures at public gatherings.
> Put your hand over your heart
> > – They dedicated themselves to follow God's commandments.
> Lift one hand in the air as if you are promising something
> > - They promised to supply all the needs for those who served daily in the
> > House of God.
> Look at your ten fingers and then your index finger
> > – One out of every ten families agreed to move back into the city.
> Now clap your hands
> > – God had done great things for Israel and even their enemies were amazed.

Practice these seven hand movements until you have the sequence. Then put the hand motions with the statements they represent.

Everyone worked together and soon the walls were done, except for the gates. The enemy became desperate and decided to kill Nehemiah. They knew they could not do this while he was inside the city, so they sent him letters asking him to meet with them in a nearby village.

He read the letter, and then sent them a message. "I am doing a great work here. Why should it stop so we can talk?"

They sent him several letters begging him to meet with them in the village. Finally they wrote a letter saying, "Everyone is talking. They are saying you are building the wall so you can rebel against the empire and make yourself king. Unless you meet with us, we are going to tell the king of Persia about your rebellion."

Nehemiah ignored their threats and continued working until the wall and the gates were finished. It took fifty-two days to complete this project, but now the city was protected.

The people rejoiced and sang praise to God. They read the Scriptures at public gatherings and dedicated themselves to follow God's commandments. They promised to supply all the needs for those who served daily in the House of God. The people who lived in the surrounding towns decided to have one out of every ten families move into the city. God had done great things for Israel, and even their enemies were amazed!

A King's Cupbearer...

- An officer of high rank who tasted the king's drink to protect him from poisoning.
- The king's cupbearer was a man who could be trusted without question.
- He was often a close confidant of the king.
- A cupbearer risked his own life every day to protect the king.

Telling the Story

NEHEMIAH

GETTING PERMISSION TO BUILD

Nehemiah served the king of Persia. He received news that his people in Judah were suffering and the walls of Jerusalem were in ruins. Sorrow overcame Nehemiah, and he sat down and cried. He was depressed for several days and prayed that God would help his people.

The king asked him why he was so sad. Nehemiah stood before him and told him about the situation in Jerusalem. The king was moved and said, "How can I help?"

"Oh please, send me to Jerusalem and give me permission to rebuild the walls."

The king said he could go, and issued letters for safe travel. Nehemiah was given access to the royal forest near Jerusalem for building materials.

Nehemiah traveled to the city and spent the first three days looking over the situation. He did not tell the people what he had in mind, but went out at night to see the city ruins. Finally he brought the leaders together and told them how God had burdened his heart. He explained how the king of Persia had given permission for rebuilding the city walls.

Nehemiah said, "We cannot live with this disgrace any longer. It is time to rebuild the walls!" All of the leaders of the land looked at one another and then enthusiastically agreed. They committed themselves to this project, and each one chose a section of the wall that would be his responsibility. They then went out and organized their people to build it.

TRYING TO STOP THE BUILDERS

The non-Jewish people of the area were angry when they saw what was happening. They decided they must try to stop the construction. They told jokes about the builders and laughed at them. They said, "These people are too weak to rebuild their city. Ha! I can see it now. They build a section of wall, and the whole thing falls down when a little fox jumps on it."

This was discouraging for the builders, but they were determined and worked faster. Soon the wall was half way up. They started joining the various sections together, which made their enemies furious. Those who opposed the building of the wall knew they had to act quickly if they were to stop the construction. They threatened to sneak up and kill the workers. They said, "We will do whatever it takes to stop this wall!"

Fear gripped the hearts of the builders, so they set up guards to watch day and night. Nehemiah encouraged them. "Don't be afraid. God is stronger than your enemies. Be prepared to fight! Fight for your fellow Jews. Fight for your sons and daughters. Fight for your wives and homes."

The workers prepared to fight from that day on. They set up a warning system in case there was an attack on any section of the wall. Men were prepared to respond quickly and rush to that area and fight.

FINISHING THE WALL

Everyone worked together and soon the walls were done, except for the gates. The enemy became desperate and decided to kill Nehemiah. They knew they could not do this while he was inside the city, so they sent him letters asking him to meet with them in a nearby village.

He read the letter, and then sent them a message. "I am doing a great work here. Why should it stop so we can talk?"

They sent him several letters begging him to meet with them in the village. Finally they wrote a letter saying, "Everyone is talking. They are saying you are building the wall so you can rebel against the empire and make yourself king. Unless you meet with us, we are going to tell the king of Persia about your rebellion."

Nehemiah ignored their threats and continued working until the wall and the gates were finished. It took fifty-two days to complete this project, but now the city was protected.

The people rejoiced and sang praise to God. They read the Scriptures at public gatherings and dedicated themselves to follow God's commandments. They promised to supply all the needs for those who served daily in the House of God. The people who lived in the surrounding towns decided to have one out of every ten families move into the city. God had done great things for Israel, and even their enemies were amazed!

Extra Storyboard

Third
Cluster

Second
Cluster

First
Cluster

Activities

Using the boxes below, give the storyboard in words or pictures.

First Cluster	Second Cluster	Third Cluster

Feel free to use blank pages to write down or draw additional clusters or ideas.

What did you learn about **God** from the story of *Nehemiah?*

_____

_____

_____

What did you learn about **people** from the story of *Nehemiah?*

_____

_____

_____

What was your **favorite** part of the story? Tell why.

_____

_____

_____

PROVERB: a pithy statement that helps you remember an important truth. Create a proverb based on this story.

_____

_____

BANNER OR BUMPER STICKER: Give the essence of this story in six words or less.

ACTIVITIES: Choose from the following, or create another activity that helps you learn the story.

Dramatic Dialogue
- Two characters – Nehemiah and one of the workers – take turns telling the various parts of this story. Emphasize the many "ups" and "downs" found in the story line.
- "The Doctor is In": One of the workers tells a psychiatrist about all the stresses and emotions involved in building the wall.

Storytelling
- Tell the story in the first person as Nehemiah. Remember he is a very emotional person!
- Group storytelling: Have several people tell the story from the perspectives of the various characters. Take turns speaking.

Art
- Draw a series of pictures to show the events of this story in the order they took place.

Group Activity
- True or False? Create a version of this story that contains at least ten false statements. Read the story to a group and ask them to shout "Stop!" when they hear something that is not true. The person who interrupts the reader must be able to correct the reader's error.

Poetry/Music
- Adapt or create a victory song expressing amazement at God's power to bring success to the wall-builders in spite of great opposition.

News Report
- "Meet the Press": Interview King Cyrus, Nehemiah, the wall builders, and an enemy of the builders.

Research
- Research the life of Ezra the scribe/priest, and prepare a report.
- Research and report on the Book of Esther, a story of the people who did not return to Judah.

Writing
- Write a newspaper article using one of the following headlines:
    CYRUS SENDS MORE JEWS BACK TO JUDAH
    WALL BUILDING MAY LEAD TO VIOLENCE
    NON-JEWS FILE PETITION WITH PERSIAN KING
    WALL PROJECT COMPLETED AFTER 52 DAYS

TIE TO PREVIOUS STORY: Write how you would connect this story with the previous story.

_____

_____

_____

TELL THE STORY: To whom did you tell the story and what was their response?

_____

_____

_____

Quiz 36

Name _____

MULTIPLE CHOICE

Date _____

____ 1. Nehemiah asked the king to send him to _____ so he could rebuild the walls of Jerusalem.
     a. Samaria   b. Canaan   c. Judah

____ 2. The king gave Nehemiah _____.
     a. 30 camels   b. letters for safe travel   c. his daughter for a wife

____ 3. He was then given access to the king's _____ near Jerusalem for building materials.
     a. palace   b. storehouse   c. forest

____ 4. When Nehemiah arrived in the city, he went out at _____ to look over the situation.
     a. daybreak   b. noon   c. night

____ 5. Finally he brought the _____ of the people together and challenged them to rebuild the wall.
     a. leaders   b. poorest   c. youngest

____ 6. The non-Jewish people who lived nearby wanted to _____ the project.
     a. stop   b. change   c. finish

____ 7. The workers prepared themselves to _____.
     a. eat   b. sleep   c. fight

____ 8. The project took them _____ from start to finish.
     a. fifty-two days   b. fifty-two weeks,   c. fifty-two years

MATCHING - People

____ 9. Artaxerxes   a. king of Persia

____ 10. Asaph   b. king's cupbearer

____ 11. Ezra   c. keeper of the king's forest

____ 12. Nehemiah   d. conspired against the builders

____ 13. Sanballat and Tobiah   e. scribe/priest who read the law of Moses to the people

MATCHING - Quotes

____ 14. "Why are you so sad?"   a. King of Persia

____ 15. "Don't be afraid…Remember the Lord."   b. Nehemiah

____ 16. "Come and meet with us in one of the villages."   c. Enemies of the Jews

____ 17. "What would you request of me?"

____ 18. "Let us build up the wall of Jerusalem."

____ 19. "If a fox goes up on their stone wall he will break it."

____ 20. "Fight for your brothers, your sons, your daughters,
     your wives, and your houses!"

(5 points each question)

SCORE _____

INTERNATIONAL
LEARNING SOLUTIONS

Dedicated to Christian Education Around the World.

BibleTelling
INTERACTIVE BIBLE LEARNING

BibleTelling has selected 36 Bible stories that give the structure of the Old Testament and teaches it in chronological order. These are divided into four books of nine stories.

BEGINNINGS

The nine stories in this first quarter tell about the beginning of the world, people, sin, crime, and a whole new beginning after the flood. They continue with the beginning of a chosen family, which is the beginning of a new nation. These stories also give God's promises to Abraham. This is a special agreement, which runs through all the Old Testament. It is important to be aware of these promises in order to understand the major themes of the Old and New Testaments.

WANDERINGS

The second quarter deals with how God's chosen family wandered away from His promised land. All of these stories involve brothers. They begin with a conflict between two brothers – Jacob and Esau – and continue with the conflict between Joseph and his brothers. Finally we see two other brothers – Moses and Aaron – working together to bring their family/nation back from their wandering and into their land.

PROMISED LAND

The third book tracks the new nation as it travels to and conquers the land God had given them. It begins with Moses leading the nation and giving them their new responsibilities and rules. He is there as they develop in character and strength before conquering the land. Joshua takes over and leads them into the land. Rahab, Ruth and Samuel all point to the shepherd/king David as he sets up the kingdom, chosen city, and chosen place of worship.

CHOSEN CITY

The last book centers around the chosen city and Temple site. This is a dramatic time in world history, as God raises up world kingdoms and mighty armies to accomplish His will. Jerusalem stands in the middle as great kings and fearless prophets come and go. Kings and kingdoms learn that God is the ruler of the entire earth.

INTERNATIONAL
LEARNING SOLUTIONS

2905 Gill Street, Bloomington, IL 61704
1-800-420-0022

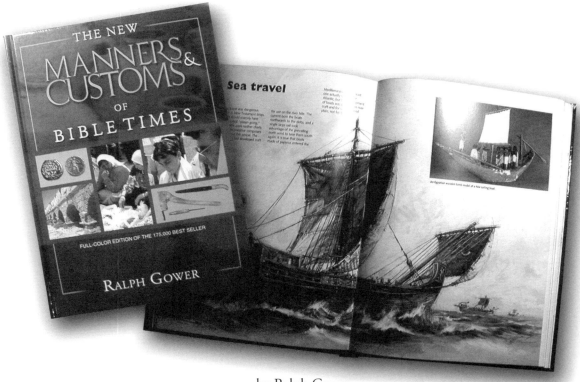